Countdown Puzzle Book 2

Also available from Granada Media Books:

Countdown Puzzle Book by
Michael Wylie and Damian Eadie

Countdown: Spreading the Word by Michael Wylie and
Damian Eadie is also available from all good bookshops
priced £9.99.

The Countdown Book of Puzzles and Games
by Michael Wylie, Damian Eadie & Robert Allen

Countdown Puzzle Book 2

By Michael Wylie and Damian Eadie

Foreword by Richard Whiteley

GRANADA

Countdown is the creation of Armond Jammot;
It is a Yorkshire Television production

First published in Great Britain in 2002
By Granada Media, an imprint of Andre Deutsch Ltd
20 Mortimer Street
London W1T 3JW

In association with Granada Media Group

ISBN 0 233 05060 4

10 9 8 7 6 5 4 3 2 1

Typeset by Derek Doyle & Associates, Liverpool
Printed and bound in the UK

Contents

Foreword

by Richard Whiteley

Hello and welcome to this monster book of *Countdown* brainteasers. What a delight! Here are pages and pages of word and number games for you to indulge in to your heart's content.

This is a good old-fashioned puzzle book. Just like the television programme, there are no gimmicks or gizmos here, we're a computer-free zone! All the games have been painstakingly worked out by Michael Wylie and Damian Eadie. Both (of course) are producers of *Countdown* and both former finalists – Michael way back in 1982, where he lost to Joyce Cansfield in Series 1, and Damian, a positive new boy, who triumphed in the final of Series 28 over Wayne Kelly in 1994.

People often call *Countdown* a quiz show but, in the strictest sense, it is not. There are no questions, merely a set of problems which require solutions. I like to call it a parlour game, in the great tradition of the programmes which were on the wireless when I was a child. Do you remember *Twenty Questions*? You had to guess an object with the help of just three clues – animal, vegetable or mineral. Or how about *Have a Go*, in which Wilfred Pickles and Mabel interviewed people in village halls all over the country? These programmes ran for years and millions tuned in.

The same can be said of television. We got a television set in 1952 (well before the Coronation which made us very posh!) and one of my earliest recollections is of tuning into *What's My Line?*. A panel of four had to guess someone's job, helped only by a simple mime act. The programme ran for years in Britain and it is still broadcast in many places all over the world. All of these programmes – all based on simple concepts – have stood the test of time. And so, I think, has *Countdown*. It retains its original look (a look we thought was trendy in 1982 but now seems positively retro) and that is the beauty of it. We won't change anything just for the sake of it. We believe that is why many millions find the programme so addictive. And because we will never run out of words or numbers – there is no reason why *Countdown* shouldn't continue to run and run. In fact, 2001 saw the first change in the format of *Countdown* when we extended the programme by 15 minutes!

When we started out in November 1982, as the first programme on Channel 4's opening night, we had been given a five-week run. Who would have thought then that we would go on to clock up 20 years and nearly 3,500 programmes? In 2002 we are still going strong, with over 3.5 million viewers each day and a contract from Channel 4 until mid-2004!

For so many of us – young and old – *Countdown* at the new time of 4.15 in the afternoon has established itself as a fixed point in our daily timetable. It's an all too brief but reliable period in which to forget the hurly burly outside and exercise our brains. For every Granny and Granddad watching there is a grandson and granddaughter, which means we are constantly replenishing our audience as the years go on. And now that there are more and more *Countdown* books, there's no need to wait until 4.15 for a daily fix!

Good luck. I warn you, these puzzles require some application and dedication. They're fun but not for the fainthearted. And if you do well and think you could have a bash at the real thing, well, who knows, we might meet up in the *Countdown* studio.

All the best,
Richard Whiteley

Introduction

So here we are – *Countdown*'s 20th year and it's still going strong. Over 1,000 weeks have passed since an incredibly youthful looking Richard Whiteley and a barely-out-of-nappies Carol Vorderman stunned the British viewing public by proving that you could have a game show which required a reasonable amount of intelligence – and still have fun.

One of the features of *Countdown* is that it is truly an interactive show; not only do our viewers play along and mark themselves against the contestants but they also send in jokes and ties for Richard, ideas for improving the show, solutions for the rare numbers game that Carol doesn't get in 30 seconds, hand-knitted dolls, Gypsy Creams, pentodes (don't ask), poems and puzzles. What would we do without them?

Hopefully this book will allow our dedicated fans to play the games in places and at times when they normally wouldn't have the chance. We received several letters after the first book which indicated that we might be reaching the right people ...

'It made the years fly by.'
Edmund Dantes (The Count of Monte Cristo)

'I woke up with it still in my hand.'
Rip Van Winkle

'I could've been a conundrum.'
Marlon Brando

… so please have fun with the enclosed word and number games and if you get stuck, don't worry – we've included the answers for no extra charge.

Michael & Damian

The rules of the game

In the programme, *Countdown* consists of 15 rounds – 11 letters games, 3 numbers games and a conundrum.

Letters games

- A contestant selects 9 letters from two piles of face-down cards (1 containing consonants, the other vowels).
- Each selection of 9 letters must contain either 3, 4 or 5 vowels, with the remainder being consonants. When the last letter has been selected, the clock is started and both contestants have 30 seconds to make the longest word they can from the letters available.
- Each letter may be used only once and only the longest word scores.
- Scoring: 1 point per letter, except for a 9-letter word – which earns 18 points.

Numbers games

- One contestant selects 6 numbers from 24 that are available. There are 4 rows to select from, the top row contains the numbers 25, 50, 75, 100; the other three rows contain the numbers 1–10 twice.
- A random 3-digit target from 100–999 is set and both contestants have 30 seconds to achieve this target, using only the four basic disciplines of addition, subtraction, multiplication and division. (No powers, fractions or decimals etc.)

- Contestants may use any or all of the numbers but may use each number only once.
- Scoring the target exactly earns 10 points. Within 5 earns 7 points and within 10 gets 5 points. Any more than 10 away from the target fails to score.

Conundrums

- A board revolves to reveal a jumbled-up 9-letter word. The contestants have to guess this 9-letter word within 30 seconds. The round is on the buzzer, and the first contestant to answer correctly gets 10 points. If a contestant gives an incorrect answer then they are excluded from any further attempts at answering and the remainder of the time is given to their opponent.

How to use this book

Letters Games

Try and make the longest word you can by using the letters in the given selection. Each letter may only be used once and you should allow yourself just 30 seconds to play each round, but if you want to take longer then please yourself. You score 1 point per letter used but you get 18 points for a 9-letter word.

Proper nouns, hyphenated words and words with capital letters are not allowed. The answers are at the back of the book, and all words given are to be found in *Countdown*'s word bible – The New Oxford Dictionary of English.

Numbers Games

You are given 6 numbers to work with that are your tools to help you reach the given target. Use any or all of the numbers but only use each number once. Only addition, multiplication, subtraction and division are allowed and you must stick to whole numbers only at all stages of your calculations – no fractions !!

Conundrum

Find the hidden 9-letter word from the letters given. A correct answer scores 10 points. As a rule of thumb, we never use 8-letter plurals as conundrums – so words like TROMBONES will never appear. All conundrums should have only one answer – but if you happen to spot a legitimate alternative then it's 10 points to you – and a rotten egg to Michael Wylie!

Hints and tips for playing *Countdown*

There is no quick guide to success when it comes to finding long words. Firstly, you must know of the word – otherwise you'll never find it in the first place, so nobody is ever going to find the longest selection in every single round, and believe me, some of these letters games are very, very tough – so if you can get maximum points one round in four, then you are doing well.

You can increase your chances of success by looking for typical word endings that are commonplace in the English language. Words ending in –iest, -er, -ing, -ted can often be found in selections; and trying to find words constructed like this is always a good way to start. Likewise, words starting with over-, out-, re- are often tucked away in there too.

Also, depending upon the letters in the selection, it can often be fruitful to pair together letters that have natural partners and see what can be made. For example, C+K, C+H, P+L etc.

Another tip is to always look out for double letters that can go together. Pairing together O, E, D, L etc. can yield some king-sized words. Remember too that the letter S is a valuable bonus that can help to make plurals, which means longer words.

Lastly, the best advice of all is that you enjoy tackling the puzzles and try to beat your own personal targets and records. So if your highest ever is a 7, strive for an 8 and then aim to repeat it. Once you think you have what it takes, write to us for an application form and then wait and see what happens.

For the conundrum, most people are of the opinion that you either see them straight away or you don't get them at all. This is not really the best way to look at it. If you can't see it after 2 seconds, then spend the next 28 or so reworking the selection to see if something comes up.

Look for endings, look for conundrums that are made up of two smaller words, and as mentioned earlier, be aware that we do not use 8-letter plurals as conundrums.

Round 1

LETTER GAME

1 | E | B | D | O | N | A | D | A | N |

| | | | | | | | | |

2 | B | R | I | T | E | N | C | Y | A |

| | | | | | | | | |

3 | T | I | T | E | N | D | I | Y | O |

| | | | | | | | | |

NUMBER GAME

| 75 | 10 | 6 | 4 | 3 | 1 | **393** |

CONUNDRUM

| A | B | A | L | D | P | A | T | E |

Round 2

LETTER GAME

1 | C | O | C | E | F | A | L | T | H |

| | | | | | | | | |

2 | C | O | M | R | A | N | I | A | T |

| | | | | | | | | |

3 | P | O | C | I | D | T | E | S | H |

| | | | | | | | | |

NUMBER GAME

| 100 | 50 | 75 | 2 | 2 | 9 | **611** |

CONUNDRUM

| R | E | D | E | E | M | N | I | T |

Round 3

LETTER GAME

1 M A N I S O L C I

2 L U B Q S R E U E

3 S M E K A N A E G

NUMBER GAME

| 50 | 8 | 10 | 1 | 3 | 8 | 555 |

CONUNDRUM

G I M E C L O W N

Round 4

LETTER GAME

1

O	B	T	R	I	L	E	C	A

2

C	R	O	H	E	A	S	R	E

3

B	U	T	I	H	E	A	D	R

NUMBER GAME

6	3	9	4	1	1	**436**

CONUNDRUM

N	I	T	E	D	E	M	O	N

Round 5

LETTER GAME

1

C	A	D	A	T	I	H	E	B

2

W	I	N	T	E	N	G	I	N

3

F	I	N	T	A	P	O	R	Y

NUMBER GAME

25	50	6	5	8	5	**735**

CONUNDRUM

I	F	B	A	L	A	N	C	E

Round 6

LETTER GAME

1 | M | A | I | L | R | O | B | E | D |

| | | | | | | | | |

2 | C | O | N | Y | B | I | S | E | T |

| | | | | | | | | |

3 | O | R | G | K | A | N | O | A | T |

| | | | | | | | | |

NUMBER GAME

| 25 | 2 | 9 | 4 | 7 | 9 | | **661** |

CONUNDRUM

| S | H | I | N | B | A | N | G | I |

6

Round 7

LETTER GAME

1 | B | E | T | S | O | A | A | G | R |

| | | | | | | | | |

2 | T | R | E | E | F | I | C | A | A |

| | | | | | | | | |

3 | C | I | S | S | T | I | D | A | R |

| | | | | | | | | |

NUMBER GAME

| 75 | 50 | 9 | 1 | 8 | 7 | **812** |

CONUNDRUM

| T | H | Y | C | A | R | E | E | R |

Round 8

LETTER GAME

1
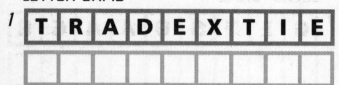

T	R	A	D	E	X	T	I	E

2

T	I	K	E	R	G	N	A	C

3

R	O	C	K	A	J	O	A	T

NUMBER GAME

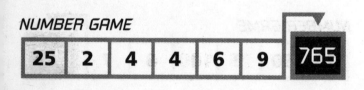

25	2	4	4	6	9	765

CONUNDRUM

D	U	E	L	F	R	E	T	S

Round 9

LETTER GAME

1

G	I	D	D	E	R	N	A	L

2

G	A	B	E	N	T	E	A	X

3

E	W	B	A	T	L	E	R	A

NUMBER GAME

50	25	75	100	6	1	**847**

CONUNDRUM

F	A	I	R	P	O	Y	N	T

Round 10

LETTER GAME

1

L	L	E	N	C	D	U	A	A

2

C	H	E	L	U	T	D	A	N

3

S	T	A	M	Y	G	N	I	C

NUMBER GAME

100	7	9	8	10	10	**304**

CONUNDRUM

T	H	I	N	G	L	O	O	M

LETTER GAME

1 C T S O E V A M Y

2 W A Y L I D E R B

3 A A D I O T R R P

NUMBER GAME

| 100 | 75 | 8 | 8 | 9 | 9 | | 939 |

CONUNDRUM

H I R E G O W N S

Round 12

LETTER GAME

1

P	O	K	S	T	D	E	A	C

2

C	U	R	R	D	E	O	P	I

3

A	R	T	I	N	S	Q	I	V

NUMBER GAME

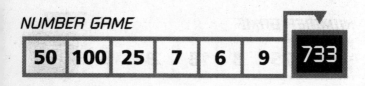

50	100	25	7	6	9	733

CONUNDRUM

L	A	D	Y	V	E	E	R	S

Round 13

LETTER GAME

1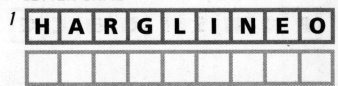

H A R G L I N E O

2

T I S E L I N W A

3

H A L D O B I S E

NUMBER GAME

25	8	3	10	2	10	**731**

CONUNDRUM

T I P S Y C H O C

Round 14

LETTER GAME

1
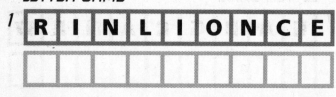

R I N L I O N C E

2

B T I H E W T I A

3
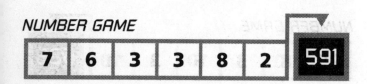

K E R L O W V A T

NUMBER GAME

| 7 | 6 | 3 | 3 | 8 | 2 | 591 |

CONUNDRUM

O U R T E M P L E

Round 15

LETTER GAME

1 `C O N T R A I A W`

2 `S L I K E D A E H`

3 `G O O N S I P S R`

NUMBER GAME

25	10	6	6	3	1	**628**

CONUNDRUM

`G R A P E L I N E`

Round 16

LETTER GAME

1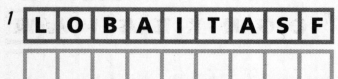

L	O	B	A	I	T	A	S	F

2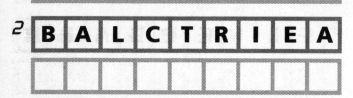

B	A	L	C	T	R	I	E	A

3

R	E	V	O	D	O	L	M	E

NUMBER GAME

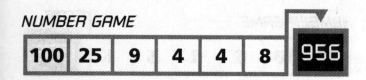

100	25	9	4	4	8	956

CONUNDRUM

G	I	A	N	T	T	I	E	S

Round 17

LETTER GAME

1 | D | R | O | K | E | B | N | W | A |

| | | | | | | | | |

2 | G | I | N | E | R | S | T | A | X |

| | | | | | | | | |

3 | B | E | R | P | T | A | O | D | W |

| | | | | | | | | |

NUMBER GAME

| 75 | 2 | 2 | 1 | 5 | 8 | **695** |

CONUNDRUM

| F | U | R | I | E | C | O | O | S |

Round 18

LETTER GAME

1 G E L T A I A T P

2 I H B E N S T A L

3 G I M A N I D E H

NUMBER GAME

| 25 | 75 | 100 | 50 | 3 | 6 | **429** |

CONUNDRUM

N E C K B L A D E

Round 19

LETTER GAME

1 | M | O | N | I | S | T | A | D | V |

| | | | | | | | | |

2 | H | O | S | L | E | F | A | O | D |

| | | | | | | | | |

3 | P | A | R | S | H | I | Y | A | R |

| | | | | | | | | |

NUMBER GAME

| 50 | 25 | 8 | 2 | 7 | 10 | **564** |

CONUNDRUM

| B | E | N | D | Y | M | O | G | I |

Round 20

LETTER GAME

1 | P | R | Y | T | E | E | A | R | A |

2 | A | N | E | E | R | U | D | S | W |

3 | B | T | Y | S | U | D | R | I | A |

NUMBER GAME

| 50 | 6 | 7 | 5 | 8 | 6 | **729** |

CONUNDRUM

| T | I | N | Y | M | E | T | A | L |

Round 21

LETTER GAME

1 | C | U | M | D | E | L | A | T | I |

2 | W | A | R | D | I | Y | E | V | J |

3 | A | L | T | T | P | E | E | R | S |

NUMBER GAME

| 75 | 25 | 2 | 9 | 2 | 6 | | **830** |

CONUNDRUM

| S | N | O | O | C | I | S | U | C |

Round 22

LETTER GAME

1 V A G I B A L E N

2 A B L O U R D E G

3 W H I D E R A P K

NUMBER GAME

| 2 | 8 | 4 | 5 | 4 | 1 | 657 |

CONUNDRUM

R I T E C I G A R

22

Round 23

LETTER GAME

1 F O O L B H E K S

⬚ ⬚ ⬚ ⬚ ⬚ ⬚ ⬚ ⬚ ⬚

2 S L I T M A N A W

⬚ ⬚ ⬚ ⬚ ⬚ ⬚ ⬚ ⬚ ⬚

3 A E R O S N I T H

⬚ ⬚ ⬚ ⬚ ⬚ ⬚ ⬚ ⬚ ⬚

NUMBER GAME

25	3	7	4	3	2	882

CONUNDRUM

R O A S T T U N A

Round 24

LETTER GAME

1 | H | U | D | E | M | O | S | A | I |

2 | M | E | T | I | L | A | C | C | A |

3 | P | O | R | R | I | M | E | S | A |

NUMBER GAME

| 75 | 5 | 1 | 6 | 6 | 1 | **542** |

CONUNDRUM

| P | O | N | I | P | R | O | G | S |

Round 25

LETTER GAME

1 | S | T | I | E | R | L | A | I | C |

| | | | | | | | | |

2 | F | I | M | P | R | E | C | A | T |

| | | | | | | | | |

3 | V | I | N | O | L | A | T | S | A |

| | | | | | | | | |

NUMBER GAME

| 50 | 25 | 9 | 2 | 5 | 7 | **828** |

CONUNDRUM

| T | I | N | Y | A | C | H | E | S |

Round 26

LETTER GAME

1 | O | D | R | I | N | A | T | O | V |

2 | A | C | D | E | E | R | S | T | E |

3 | T | U | N | A | T | I | Q | Y | N |

NUMBER GAME

| 50 | 25 | 75 | 3 | 1 | 2 | **407** |

CONUNDRUM

| S | P | E | E | D | C | U | T | S |

Round 27

LETTER GAME

1 | A | R | R | W | E | D | R | A | T |

| | | | | | | | | |

2 | R | E | C | S | T | O | O | E | S |

| | | | | | | | | |

3 | G | A | L | I | T | O | B | E | R |

| | | | | | | | | |

NUMBER GAME

| 25 | 9 | 1 | 4 | 5 | 6 | | **848** |

CONUNDRUM

| C | A | B | I | N | T | O | U | R |

Round 28

LETTER GAME

1 `D` `R` `U` `I` `I` `F` `E` `P` `F`

2 `A` `N` `I` `G` `E` `R` `D` `A` `T`

3 `F` `I` `N` `L` `A` `D` `E` `S` `S`

NUMBER GAME

50	4	6	10	1	7	**972**

CONUNDRUM

`G` `R` `A` `N` `D` `P` `I` `N` `E`

Round 29

LETTER GAME

1 | B | L | O | N | E | A | M | E | T |
|---|---|---|---|---|---|---|---|---|
| | | | | | | | | |

2 | L | I | K | C | P | I | R | E | R |
|---|---|---|---|---|---|---|---|---|
| | | | | | | | | |

3 | B | O | R | T | I | O | G | N | E |
|---|---|---|---|---|---|---|---|---|
| | | | | | | | | |

NUMBER GAME

50	100	1	10	10	1	**630**

CONUNDRUM

M	O	T	O	R	P	O	N	I

Round 30

LETTER GAME

1

R	O	D	L	D	A	N	L	E

2

S	C	U	T	O	I	C	A	W

3

K	I	R	E	S	S	T	A	W

NUMBER GAME

100	75	25	2	4	2		683

CONUNDRUM

F	O	R	R	H	E	I	D	I

30

Round 31

LETTER GAME

1

D	I	L	L	E	N	T	A	C

2

C	R	E	P	O	T	I	N	E

3

H	O	G	I	T	U	D	E	S

NUMBER GAME

25	100	7	7	4	3	578

CONUNDRUM

W	A	R	N	S	E	R	I	C

Round 32

LETTER GAME

1
Y O V E L S A S T

2
L A P P O R E S I

3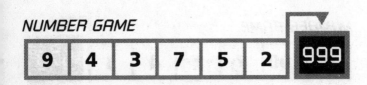
L N I H T A F G E

NUMBER GAME

9 4 3 7 5 2 | 999

CONUNDRUM

N O T E D M A I D

Round 33

LETTER GAME

1 D A V E P I J T A

2 L I S T E A C S B

3 C U S L I R V E E

NUMBER GAME

| 25 | 75 | 50 | 100 | 8 | 7 | **942** |

CONUNDRUM

L U N A D I N G O

Round 34

LETTER GAME

1

D	I	L	T	E	R	E	B	S

2

M	M	I	T	U	R	E	A	E

3

S	L	A	C	E	T	O	B	W

NUMBER GAME

100	7	10	9	10	1	**244**

CONUNDRUM

D	E	V	I	L	D	A	T	A

Round 35

LETTER GAME

1 | C | O | N | E | J | A | T | D | K |

| | | | | | | | | |

2 | T | H | O | R | O | S | P | A | C |

| | | | | | | | | |

3 | T | R | U | S | I | C | E | R | Q |

| | | | | | | | | |

NUMBER GAME

| 50 | 75 | 25 | 5 | 5 | 1 | 386 |

CONUNDRUM

| F | I | N | D | G | O | Y | I | M |

Round 36

LETTER GAME

1

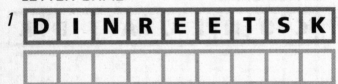

D I N R E E T S K

2

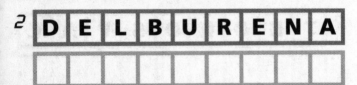

D E L B U R E N A

3

D O R R P A T E A

NUMBER GAME

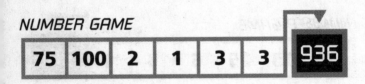

| 75 | 100 | 2 | 1 | 3 | 3 | **936** |

CONUNDRUM

R A C I E T E X T

Round 37

LETTER GAME

1 | H | O | N | C | O | R | E | S | P |

2 | D | E | R | N | O | M | A | T | N |

3 | U | N | T | R | A | L | T | A | A |

NUMBER GAME

| 25 | 75 | 100 | 10 | 10 | 9 | **416** |

CONUNDRUM

| U | C | R | Y | S | A | N | T | A |

LETTER GAME

1 | S | O | N | D | E | M | A | H | I |

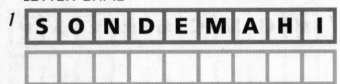

2 | H | U | N | D | R | E | N | A | D |

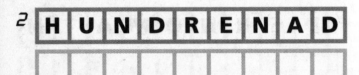

3 | A | B | C | D | E | I | O | U | V |

NUMBER GAME

| 25 | 2 | 3 | 8 | 3 | 6 | **667** |

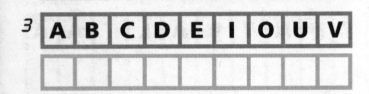

CONUNDRUM

| L | I | L | Y | Q | U | O | O | S |

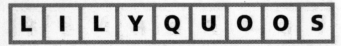

Round 39

LETTER GAME

1 | N | I | F | A | N | C | E | R | E |

| | | | | | | | | |

2 | C | O | D | I | M | A | G | T | U |

| | | | | | | | | |

3 | C | H | E | E | P | A | R | D | I |

| | | | | | | | | |

NUMBER GAME

| 2 | 5 | 9 | 8 | 9 | 4 | **570** |

CONUNDRUM

| I | D | I | F | E | R | R | E | T |

Round 40

LETTER GAME

1 R A M I S T I C Y

2 O C B T R A I A E

3 D E O O T A T T N

NUMBER GAME

75	25	1	10	4	4	841

CONUNDRUM

M A G I C T R A P

Round 41

LETTER GAME

1 C H E A R U P S C

2 P E L B K E A E R

3 S E M I N A T G E

NUMBER GAME

50	25	8	7	7	5	**543**

CONUNDRUM

T O P R I N G E R

Round 42

LETTER GAME

1 X U U B R Y P E A

2 B L U F E T A R E

3 P O M E U S N Y O

NUMBER GAME

| 8 | 3 | 4 | 2 | 10 | 9 | **734** |

CONUNDRUM

A N O I N T E S S

Round 43

LETTER GAME

1 G E R V I N A Q U

2 R I G U T I S T A

3 A R C U I L D E T

NUMBER GAME

| 100 | 9 | 5 | 8 | 7 | 9 | **643** |

CONUNDRUM

F A N C E E F U L

Round 44

LETTER GAME

1

C U L P I T O E M

2

S P E N T O L A W

3

R E Q O R N U C O

NUMBER GAME

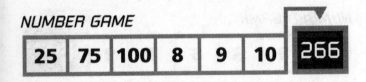

| 25 | 75 | 100 | 8 | 9 | 10 | 266 |

CONUNDRUM

T O E D A N G L E

44

Round 45

LETTER GAME

1 G I O L I N E R A

2 O X E D L S I Y C

3 H A R M F D A E N

NUMBER GAME

| 50 | 7 | 5 | 7 | 2 | 4 | 820 |

CONUNDRUM

S T A R T O P E R

Round 46

LETTER GAME

1 U R I N C A P S G

2 S U R G L E B A S

3 C R O S T P A D U

NUMBER GAME

| 75 | 6 | 10 | 4 | 3 | 2 | **538** |

CONUNDRUM

D I N A M I T T E

Round 47

LETTER GAME

1 | V | I | R | B | U | S | O | T | E |

| | | | | | | | | |

2 | P | O | A | L | E | J | A | N | W |

| | | | | | | | | |

3 | M | A | R | G | E | D | N | E | D |

| | | | | | | | | |

NUMBER GAME

| 50 | 75 | 4 | 4 | 2 | 2 | **776** |

CONUNDRUM

| N | I | G | H | T | B | E | A | R |

Round 48

LETTER GAME

1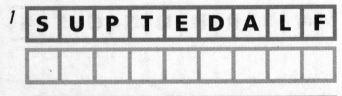

S	U	P	T	E	D	A	L	F

2

F	R	A	C	T	E	R	A	E

3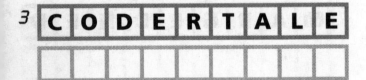

C	O	D	E	R	T	A	L	E

NUMBER GAME

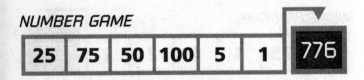

25	75	50	100	5	1	776

CONUNDRUM

M	A	C	A	R	O	N	I	P

Round 49

LETTER GAME

1

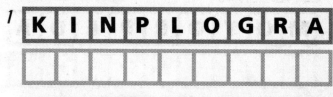

K	I	N	P	L	O	G	R	A

2

M	E	D	E	S	A	C	R	U

3

G	I	N	T	I	C	E	S	B

NUMBER GAME

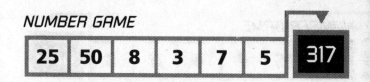

25	50	8	3	7	5		317

CONUNDRUM

D	I	G	S	D	U	E	T	S

49

Round 50

LETTER GAME

1

M	O	T	O	R	P	E	D	A

2

S	M	O	R	K	I	G	A	S

3

T	U	N	R	I	C	S	Y	O

NUMBER GAME

100	25	7	4	1	8	629

CONUNDRUM

P	A	M	E	L	I	T	I	C

Round 51

LETTER GAME

1 D Y P O L E M E R

2 A R R I P D E E H

3 C U R G A N L I E

NUMBER GAME

| 10 | 1 | 6 | 7 | 8 | 5 | 841 |

CONUNDRUM

N I T R O F O A M

Round 52

LETTER GAME

1 R I M E D I A L A

2 B E D R I E S A F

3 G L A N E D C O E

NUMBER GAME

| 75 | 5 | 3 | 6 | 8 | 4 | **760** |

CONUNDRUM

T H R E E D A V S

Round 53

LETTER GAME

1 S I N C D R E E E

2 C R I D T E M I H

3 C H U N D E A L R

NUMBER GAME

| 75 | 100 | 2 | 3 | 4 | 9 | **844** |

CONUNDRUM

S E E S B L A N K

Round 54

LETTER GAME

1 O N I F E S H A D

2 V I R E S T E C E

3 C A I N S T S E N

NUMBER GAME

25	5	2	1	7	3	**782**

CONUNDRUM

N I N O R O U G H

Round 55

LETTER GAME

1 G U S T I P E D O

2 A A B G E L I R C

3 O U T L E R S U T

NUMBER GAME

| 50 | 100 | 25 | 75 | 4 | 4 | **693** |

CONUNDRUM

T O T U N I S I A

Round 56

LETTER GAME

1 F I L D O M A N D

2 D E T E N C I C O

3 D E I T A S V E H

NUMBER GAME

| 75 | 50 | 25 | 8 | 2 | 3 | 927 |

CONUNDRUM

B U N D U T O E D

Round 57

LETTER GAME

1

A	R	T	E	N	G	E	E	H

2

Q	U	E	B	I	Z	E	T	P

3

P	E	L	U	D	C	A	N	S

NUMBER GAME

75	4	6	6	5	3	849

CONUNDRUM

A	L	E	E	B	A	R	G	E

Round 58

LETTER GAME

1 D I J A N C E U R

2 C E T O L L A D A

3 M I N R A P Z A E

NUMBER GAME

50	75	5	3	4	4	**726**

CONUNDRUM

N I C K S Q U A D

Round 59

LETTER GAME

1 M U T I Q E E S U

2 E E N B I R G D A

3 T U L L P E D O N

NUMBER GAME

| 50 | 8 | 7 | 2 | 1 | 4 | **689** |

CONUNDRUM

L O U S Y R I S E

Round 60

LETTER GAME

1

A	R	C	U	S	T	E	A	C

2

Y	A	C	I	L	L	B	N	U

3

N	O	T	I	S	Q	U	E	H

NUMBER GAME

6	3	8	8	3	7	**941**

CONUNDRUM

S	O	N	I	C	L	U	N	I

Round 61

LETTER GAME

1

N	N	H	O	P	R	L	A	E

2

T	H	E	I	R	G	A	W	N

3

D	I	S	P	O	M	R	E	C

NUMBER GAME

100	7	5	3	9	6	237

CONUNDRUM

H	E	D	G	R	I	N	D	S

Round 62

LETTER GAME

1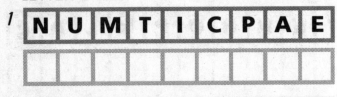

N	U	M	T	I	C	P	A	E

2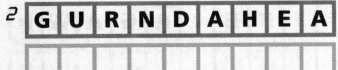

G	U	R	N	D	A	H	E	A

3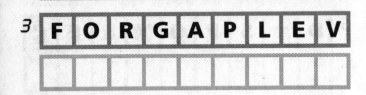

F	O	R	G	A	P	L	E	V

NUMBER GAME

50	6	5	7	9	4		679

CONUNDRUM

N	O	S	E	S	H	R	U	G

Round 63

LETTER GAME

1

A	L	M	E	N	T	I	U	C

2

Y	I	N	T	O	R	S	I	E

3

P	R	R	E	D	A	T	U	E

NUMBER GAME

50	75	4	4	8	2		547

CONUNDRUM

T	A	G	O	R	I	L	L	A

Round 64

LETTER GAME

1

A	N	R	A	T	T	E	R	D

2

T	R	O	M	A	E	G	E	S

3

G	H	O	U	P	L	E	D	N

NUMBER GAME

75	50	25	5	4	4	637

CONUNDRUM

R	A	P	R	A	P	H	A	G

LETTER GAME

1 S A R B E I S R E

2 H U B C L O U S E

3 G L A R I O S E F

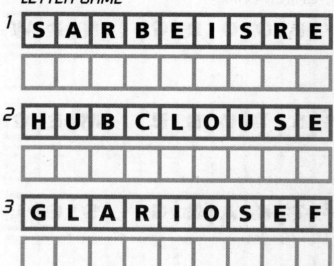

NUMBER GAME

| 100 | 3 | 6 | 2 | 2 | 1 | 555 |

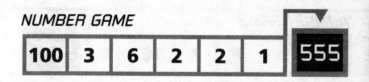

CONUNDRUM

W E T B O I N G S

Round 66

LETTER GAME

1 | F | O | O | R | G | I | N | P | W |

| | | | | | | | | |

2 | S | T | U | R | N | I | M | E | O |

| | | | | | | | | |

3 | T | R | A | N | G | I | S | E | J |

| | | | | | | | | |

NUMBER GAME

| 25 | 9 | 7 | 2 | 10 | 1 | | 585 |

CONUNDRUM

| C | L | I | F | F | D | U | T | I |

66

Round 67

LETTER GAME

1

A	G	I	L	L	P	E	X	S

2

E	M	M	L	I	S	T	A	C

3

R	A	S	S	A	M	C	E	T

NUMBER GAME

6	7	10	8	3	8	**592**

CONUNDRUM

C	O	L	D	E	R	T	E	A

Round 68

LETTER GAME

1 B A T S H E B I S

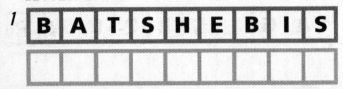

2 C H O R E T I P P

3 C T R O K E S A I

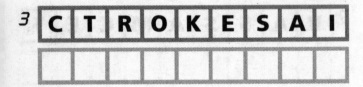

NUMBER GAME

| 75 | 50 | 100 | 25 | 9 | 8 | 360 |

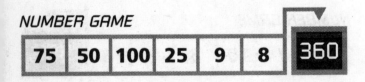

CONUNDRUM

A L P I N H E R D

Round 69

LETTER GAME

1 C R E T I G A N R

2 U N D E N O C E X

3 W O H E K D S A N

NUMBER GAME

75 25 4 8 9 7 **978**

CONUNDRUM

E A T I N G R I O

LETTER GAME

1 | T | H | O | O | B | S | E | A | U |

2 | B | I | W | S | I | N | G | N | E |

3 | M | O | N | N | E | L | B | A | F |

NUMBER GAME

| 100 | 75 | 50 | 10 | 9 | 8 | **944** |

CONUNDRUM

| N | I | C | K | E | R | B | I | G |

Round 71

LETTER GAME

1

L	W	E	G	I	N	C	A	R

2

C	L	O	M	I	B	S	H	A

3

H	I	N	B	E	T	I	A	D

NUMBER GAME

25	3	4	8	10	10	**615**

CONUNDRUM

S	E	E	B	L	O	N	D	E

Round 72

LETTER GAME

1 | W | R | I | D | E | B | L | E | T |

2 | L | U | R | I | C | A | S | T | O |

3 | Y | E | O | J | A | P | R | D | E |

NUMBER GAME

| 75 | 9 | 9 | 1 | 2 | 1 | **732** |

CONUNDRUM

| C | R | I | M | A | T | I | O | N |

Round 73

LETTER GAME

1

S	O	L	I	N	F	E	E	T

2

S	T	E	R	A	T	O	P	M

3

S	M	I	S	O	T	L	I	A

NUMBER GAME

100	50	6	4	1	5	783

CONUNDRUM

D	A	T	E	G	U	A	R	D

Round 74

LETTER GAME

1 | S | U | S | O | D | E | L | R | O |

| | | | | | | | | |

2 | C | H | P | O | R | I | U | E | G |

| | | | | | | | | |

3 | S | P | U | L | I | T | A | Y | W |

| | | | | | | | | |

NUMBER GAME

| 100 | 75 | 50 | 25 | 7 | 7 | **918** |

CONUNDRUM

| O | C | E | A | N | W | A | L | L |

Round 75

LETTER GAME

1 | H | O | S | R | M | A | C | K | E |

| | | | | | | | | |

2 | S | H | O | R | P | Y | A | D | I |

| | | | | | | | | |

3 | T | R | O | B | A | G | E | M | H |

| | | | | | | | | |

NUMBER GAME

| 9 | 3 | 10 | 10 | 7 | 5 | | **854** |

CONUNDRUM

| S | E | C | O | N | N | D | E | D |

Round 76

LETTER GAME

1 S P U Q I T E C K

2 M O N D E L A E T

3 F L I H E N G S O

NUMBER GAME

| 100 | 50 | 25 | 7 | 6 | 1 | 823 |

CONUNDRUM

P E R S I L A D S

Round 77

LETTER GAME

1 E X P I N C E L R

2 C L U N I P A B Q

3 C E N T O L U E S

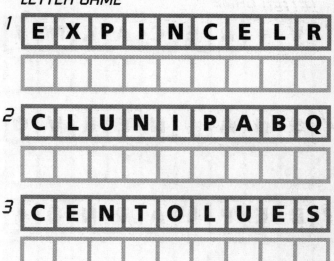

NUMBER GAME

| 25 | 2 | 3 | 3 | 1 | 1 | **648** |

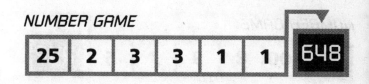

CONUNDRUM

I N V E R N O G G

77

Round 78

LETTER GAME

1

V	I	R	E	C	A	K	M	T

2

S	H	A	I	N	E	R	V	O

3

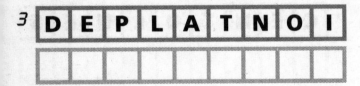

D	E	P	L	A	T	N	O	I

NUMBER GAME

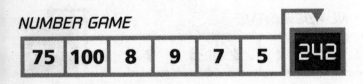

75	100	8	9	7	5	242

CONUNDRUM

G	R	A	P	H	I	B	O	Y

Round 79

LETTER GAME

1 G R I B S A M R E

2 T H I S T E R I S

3 B I R D S H U F E

NUMBER GAME

| 75 | 6 | 8 | 3 | 2 | 8 | 993 |

CONUNDRUM

I N D I E T O G S

Round 80

LETTER GAME

1 F E I O L D I L P

2 D O N S A B E N I

3 Z T B O N E A E G

NUMBER GAME

100	6	7	7	8	8	**376**

CONUNDRUM

L Y R I C A L D O

Round 81

LETTER GAME

1

W	A	I	K	E	R	T	N	R

2

S	T	E	M	N	A	T	E	T

3

L	A	S	I	D	U	E	N	T

NUMBER GAME

25	3	1	6	9	8	722

CONUNDRUM

T	I	L	L	B	I	N	G	E

Round 82

LETTER GAME

1 | H | I | R | R | E | D | I | P | S |

2 | S | C | T | E | L | M | A | S | A |

3 | T | O | L | H | H | I | S | E | W |

NUMBER GAME

| 100 | 25 | 2 | 8 | 10 | 8 | **749** |

CONUNDRUM

| T | O | N | E | D | C | I | C | E |

Round 83

LETTER GAME

1 | R | I | N | T | E | L | E | J | H |

| | | | | | | | | |

2 | T | E | N | B | E | A | U | N | P |

| | | | | | | | | |

3 | G | U | D | D | E | R | P | A | I |

| | | | | | | | | |

NUMBER GAME

| 25 | 1 | 3 | 5 | 1 | 7 | **444** |

CONUNDRUM

| S | C | O | T | I | A | S | E | A |

Round 84

LETTER GAME

1

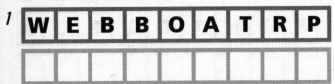

W	E	B	B	O	A	T	R	P

2

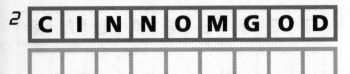

C	I	N	N	O	M	G	O	D

3

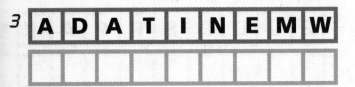

A	D	A	T	I	N	E	M	W

NUMBER GAME

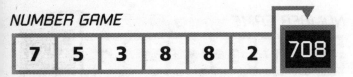

7	5	3	8	8	2	**708**

CONUNDRUM

G	I	N	G	E	R	T	U	T

Round 85

LETTER GAME

1

T	O	M	P	O	L	R	L	I

2

D	O	C	H	T	A	R	E	B

3

B	O	L	E	P	C	A	O	W

NUMBER GAME

75	9	8	2	10	1	355

CONUNDRUM

B	E	L	L	A	M	A	L	E

Round 86

LETTER GAME

1

B	S	H	E	O	L	K	A	C

2

D	E	N	T	H	I	G	L	E

3

D	L	R	O	B	E	V	U	A

NUMBER GAME

25	50	2	9	4	7	**934**

CONUNDRUM

R	I	O	M	O	W	E	R	S

Round 87

LETTER GAME

1 T H O S E P W A S

2 T A M I L E A E F

3 T H O R E C A K S

NUMBER GAME

100	75	25	8	10	2	469

CONUNDRUM

T O T A L I N F O

Round 88

LETTER GAME

1

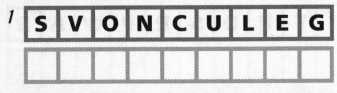

S	V	O	N	C	U	L	E	G

2

C	O	R	T	I	P	A	S	Y

3

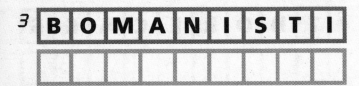

B	O	M	A	N	I	S	T	I

NUMBER GAME

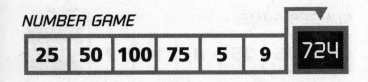

25	50	100	75	5	9	**724**

CONUNDRUM

F	I	N	E	S	T	G	I	N

LETTER GAME

1 F E L U D A T E D

2 C O G N A L I T S

3 D O O W E R S O N

NUMBER GAME

| 50 | 6 | 8 | 4 | 4 | 2 | **333** |

CONUNDRUM

P I N C O S U S I

Round 90

LETTER GAME

1 H Y C A L L E B E

2 H U L F E S F D I

3 M E S A N G E R D

NUMBER GAME

| 50 | 7 | 1 | 6 | 3 | 7 | 827 |

CONUNDRUM

N E A T P E T E R

Round 91

LETTER GAME

1 | S | T | H | I | R | K | C | E | A |

2 | A | B | S | D | P | R | E | D | E |

3 | P | E | N | C | O | S | T | O | R |

NUMBER GAME

| 25 | 7 | 7 | 6 | 5 | 9 | | 342 |

CONUNDRUM

| O | V | A | L | T | E | E | N | I |

Round 92

LETTER GAME

1

T	T	E	E	P	P	I	S	L

2

M	O	U	N	I	S	L	E	I

3

M	O	R	O	K	I	S	C	E

NUMBER GAME

75	25	3	3	5	7	**659**

CONUNDRUM

U	N	I	S	O	R	T	I	N

Round 93

LETTER GAME

1
I	N	D	U	R	B	E	S	T

2
A	L	C	H	T	I	N	E	O

3
C	H	I	R	A	D	L	E	O

NUMBER GAME

100	50	25	7	5	4	333

CONUNDRUM

K	I	N	D	E	R	N	A	G

Round 94

LETTER GAME

1

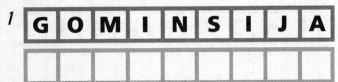

G	O	M	I	N	S	I	J	A

2

C	H	E	B	L	E	A	M	Z

3

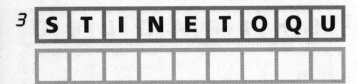

S	T	I	N	E	T	O	Q	U

NUMBER GAME

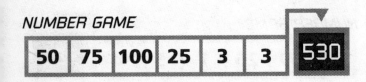

50	75	100	25	3	3		530

CONUNDRUM

J	O	E	L	Y	B	E	A	N

Round 95

LETTER GAME

1 | V | I | O | N | I | A | S | N | P |

2 | S | L | O | T | F | E | C | K | I |

3 | H | I | R | W | A | R | S | E | T |

NUMBER GAME

| 100 | 6 | 9 | 3 | 4 | 8 | | 678 |

CONUNDRUM

| F | U | R | S | T | L | E | S | S |

Round 96

LETTER GAME

1

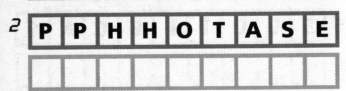

O	L	O	N	C	A	D	E	Y

2

P	P	H	H	O	T	A	S	E

3

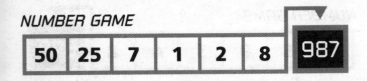

D	E	P	I	S	T	E	S	A

NUMBER GAME

50	25	7	1	2	8	987

CONUNDRUM

E	A	G	L	E	T	E	D	D

Round 97

LETTER GAME

1

T	H	O	M	A	S	T	E	Y

2

Z	E	P	I	T	M	O	I	C

3

C	H	E	N	I	A	M	S	R

NUMBER GAME

7	9	10	5	10	7	842

CONUNDRUM

I	C	E	F	A	U	S	T	O

Round 98

LETTER GAME

1

C	A	N	V	O	B	I	E	C

2

F	E	N	S	T	A	B	E	A

3

M	I	N	G	S	R	E	I	P

NUMBER GAME

100	2	4	8	6	2	777

CONUNDRUM

M	A	R	I	E	S	W	O	E

Round 99

LETTER GAME

1 L E R U O T E L G

2 S H E R I T O S E

3 S C R O K C W E R

NUMBER GAME

| 25 | 1 | 7 | 4 | 2 | 3 | **830** |

CONUNDRUM

N A T I V E D I C

Round 100

LETTER GAME

1

D	E	R	N	I	H	A	L	P

2

K	O	L	D	W	E	G	E	N

3

P	R	O	C	H	E	A	N	E

NUMBER GAME

100	75	8	3	5	9	**441**

CONUNDRUM

N	E	C	K	B	I	N	G	O

Round 101

LETTER GAME

1 A C D E E I L U T

2 M R U O S I N G O

3 S N N A I M E L T

NUMBER GAME

75 5 1 7 3 5 666

CONUNDRUM

D E E P R I V A L

Round 102

LETTER GAME

1 H V C O N A I S E

2 C I R E N S T I Y

3 P R E K I B U S I

NUMBER GAME

50	100	4	5	4	5	685

CONUNDRUM

S T R A Y M O O N

Round 103

LETTER GAME

1 Y T H I M A N G E

2 Y T N O B E A D E

3 E X P O R D I E U

NUMBER GAME

| 75 | 2 | 10 | 10 | 5 | 7 | **468** |

CONUNDRUM

L I F T A C O I N

Round 104

LETTER GAME

1 L A T E S E L K O

2 M T R E I C O S I

3 D E T O P I A V E

NUMBER GAME

| 25 | 100 | 6 | 4 | 5 | 2 | **880** |

CONUNDRUM

S U G A R I C O N

Round 105

LETTER GAME

1

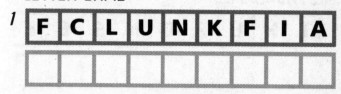

F	C	L	U	N	K	F	I	A

2

B	U	D	R	A	N	I	S	E

3

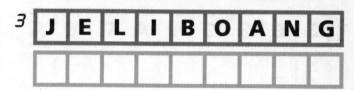

J	E	L	I	B	O	A	N	G

NUMBER GAME

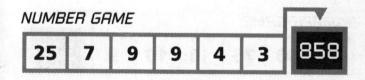

25	7	9	9	4	3	858

CONUNDRUM

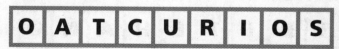

O	A	T	C	U	R	I	O	S

Round 106

LETTER GAME

1

T H U P O N S E E

2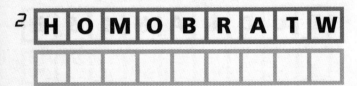

H O M O B R A T W

3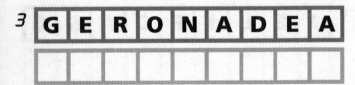

G E R O N A D E A

NUMBER GAME

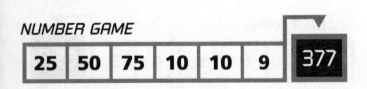

| 25 | 50 | 75 | 10 | 10 | 9 | 377 |

CONUNDRUM

I B I T E H A N D

Round 107

LETTER GAME

1 | D | E | N | H | O | M | A | T | E |

2 | T | I | A | L | P | O | C | S | W |

3 | C | K | U | L | P | A | L | S | I |

NUMBER GAME

| 50 | 100 | 4 | 3 | 1 | 8 | | 634 |

CONUNDRUM

| N | O | L | U | N | A | T | I | C |

Round 108

LETTER GAME

1 | Z | A | I | D | L | V | R | O | S |

| | | | | | | | | |

2 | W | I | N | E | V | A | R | B | A |

| | | | | | | | | |

3 | F | O | B | E | R | O | S | W | U |

| | | | | | | | | |

NUMBER GAME

| 8 | 3 | 10 | 7 | 6 | 1 | **909** |

CONUNDRUM

| I | N | T | O | M | A | N | I | A |

Round 109

LETTER GAME

1

I	N	G	A	H	I	T	Y	N

2

H	O	P	I	N	E	R	W	S

3

D	U	N	I	T	E	F	I	L

NUMBER GAME

50	10	9	2	3	1	706

CONUNDRUM

G	A	N	G	L	I	L	I	P

Round 110

LETTER GAME

1 L E S P I A N E C

2 P H O M I N C A W

3 R O M O C E K S A

NUMBER GAME

| 75 | 8 | 6 | 10 | 2 | 4 | **999** |

CONUNDRUM

B L E E D T A N K

Round 111

LETTER GAME

1 | B | L | U | N | I | M | A | T | H |

| | | | | | | | | |

2 | O | L | D | E | D | B | A | T | P |

| | | | | | | | | |

3 | L | E | C | R | A | D | U | T | E |

| | | | | | | | | |

NUMBER GAME

| 75 | 50 | 100 | 6 | 2 | 9 | | 421 |

CONUNDRUM

| M | O | O | T | A | L | I | E | N |

Round 112

LETTER GAME

1 | B | R | I | N | T | E | A | H | E |

| | | | | | | | | |

2 | R | R | R | I | S | B | T | E | A |

| | | | | | | | | |

3 | M | I | S | T | R | E | M | A | S |

| | | | | | | | | |

NUMBER GAME

| 25 | 75 | 100 | 1 | 3 | 1 | **882** |

CONUNDRUM

| L | O | C | A | L | D | A | T | E |

Round 113

LETTER GAME

1 | O | K | A | P | E | B | O | E | X |

| | | | | | | | | |

2 | F | I | D | N | E | L | I | M | E |

| | | | | | | | | |

3 | S | E | M | I | C | T | L | A | E |

| | | | | | | | | |

NUMBER GAME

| 25 | 10 | 7 | 9 | 9 | 2 | **931** |

CONUNDRUM

| I | D | O | L | I | S | E | U | R |

Round 114

LETTER GAME

1

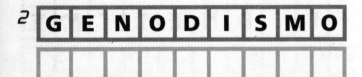

A	A	C	E	P	U	L	S	T

2

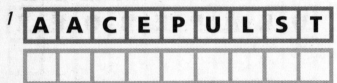

G	E	N	O	D	I	S	M	O

3

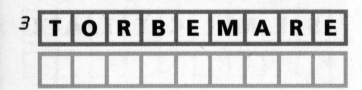

T	O	R	B	E	M	A	R	E

NUMBER GAME

100	2	2	5	1	10	784

CONUNDRUM

G	R	E	A	T	P	I	N	T

Round 115

LETTER GAME

1 D R N E W A N D E

2 L U T O M A D E Q

3 C U T N I V O S R

NUMBER GAME

| 25 | 50 | 9 | 4 | 3 | 2 | | **998** |

CONUNDRUM

T E M P L E D O C

Round 116

LETTER GAME

1 S I N C U A S E R

2 T E D I S P U C A

3 A B D A T I O N Y

NUMBER GAME

| 10 | 7 | 9 | 7 | 8 | 10 | **621** |

CONUNDRUM

S U P E R D O O N

Round 117

LETTER GAME

1 | H | O | M | O | D | E | C | S | I |

2 | M | E | R | N | U | A | S | E | Y |

3 | S | Y | U | N | R | E | O | J | D |

NUMBER GAME

| 50 | 25 | 10 | 4 | 8 | 3 | **319** |

CONUNDRUM

| C | A | V | I | N | G | D | A | N |

Round 118

LETTER GAME

1 S O D E P L A E B

2 S P U I N B E S M

3 W O R N I D E E D

NUMBER GAME

| 25 | 3 | 9 | 6 | 5 | 6 | **611** |

CONUNDRUM

C A S E D T H I S

Round 119

LETTER GAME

1 L I R G A N S N O

2 S T A L I Y O R T

3 W I T H F E C S O

NUMBER GAME

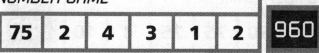

75 2 4 3 1 2 **960**

CONUNDRUM

T E N D E R T I M

Round 120

LETTER GAME

1 | O | R | N | O | D | E | T | A | S |

| | | | | | | | | |

2 | T | E | R | I | N | C | A | Y | T |

| | | | | | | | | |

3 | M | E | N | T | E | P | V | A | I |

| | | | | | | | | |

NUMBER GAME

| 100 | 50 | 75 | 25 | 4 | 10 | **283** |

CONUNDRUM

| S | U | P | E | R | D | E | A | D |

Round 121

LETTER GAME

1

H	I	G	N	O	L	R	A	W

2

G	U	N	I	L	T	O	V	A

3

S	O	L	D	I	A	G	N	S

NUMBER GAME

25	8	2	3	10	7	645

CONUNDRUM

H	O	T	E	L	C	O	C	A

Round 122

LETTER GAME

1

2

3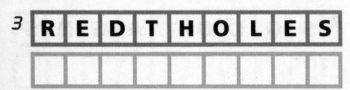

NUMBER GAME

50	75	4	6	5	3	**802**

CONUNDRUM

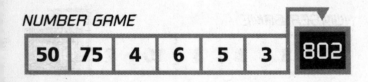

S I M M E R S E E

Round 123

LETTER GAME

1

G	R	L	A	B	E	P	O	E

2

W	E	L	I	N	G	T	O	N

3

D	R	O	S	W	P	S	A	U

NUMBER GAME

100	10	9	1	2	2	933

CONUNDRUM

T	E	D	R	A	V	E	R	S

Round 124

LETTER GAME

1

F	W	O	N	A	L	L	S	E

2

A	T	T	C	E	N	R	O	I

3

S	C	O	M	A	R	I	G	S

NUMBER GAME

75	100	50	6	3	9	781

CONUNDRUM

G	R	A	N	D	P	I	E	S

Round 125

LETTER GAME

1 | I | V | E | L | I | M | O | C | A |

2 | M | O | N | G | I | L | A | F | P |

3 | T | E | B | G | U | N | A | S | I |

NUMBER GAME

| 8 | 5 | 3 | 1 | 4 | 2 | **522** |

CONUNDRUM

| R | U | D | E | C | E | L | T | S |

Round 126

LETTER GAME

1

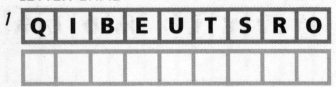

Q	I	B	E	U	T	S	R	O

2

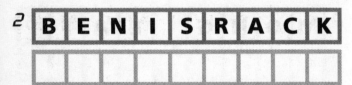

B	E	N	I	S	R	A	C	K

3

S	N	O	F	F	I	U	E	P

NUMBER GAME

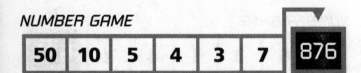

50	10	5	4	3	7	876

CONUNDRUM

T	E	A	B	R	E	A	T	H

Round 127

LETTER GAME

1 | S | Q | U | E | R | P | A | T | D |

2 | P | H | E | R | I | M | O | N | K |

3 | A | L | B | I | S | T | A | P | M |

NUMBER GAME

| 25 | 2 | 3 | 4 | 1 | 4 | **619** |

CONUNDRUM

| R | E | N | D | C | H | I | N | A |

Round 128

LETTER GAME

1 F O T E K A C B S

2 D A M E R T A S N

3 B H O R O S A D A

NUMBER GAME

| 100 | 75 | 5 | 3 | 7 | 7 | 616 |

CONUNDRUM

G I N P O T T I E

Round 129

LETTER GAME

1

D	R	O	B	E	L	I	A	P

2

R	E	M	O	R	B	O	S	T

3

A	C	D	I	N	O	S	T	U

NUMBER GAME

25	100	75	50	6	8	**222**

CONUNDRUM

I	N	C	A	F	I	N	A	L

Round 130

LETTER GAME

1 | G | U | R | Y | V | E | O | A | F |

| | | | | | | | | |

2 | R | O | E | L | I | S | T | E | T |

| | | | | | | | | |

3 | B | U | B | S | T | I | E | T | S |

| | | | | | | | | |

NUMBER GAME

| 50 | 3 | 4 | 2 | 9 | 9 | **999** |

CONUNDRUM

| R | O | C | S | W | R | E | C | K |

Round 131

LETTER GAME

1

Q	E	N	T	A	B	U	D	E

2

G	A	R	D	I	P	A	L	E

3

T	R	A	M	N	E	U	E	Y

NUMBER GAME

75	100	6	1	7	5	**859**

CONUNDRUM

S	N	O	B	D	U	E	L	S

Round 132

LETTER GAME

1

O C T U S E P L R

2

G O N I L A H O W

3

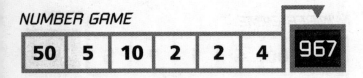

H A R P O N E D T

NUMBER GAME

| 50 | 5 | 10 | 2 | 2 | 4 | 967 |

CONUNDRUM

D D E E R H U N T

Round 133

LETTER GAME

1 U M O S E T A L P

2 X I D E F O Y T C

3 D I N N U G O S R

NUMBER GAME

| 2 | 7 | 10 | 3 | 4 | 4 | 672 |

CONUNDRUM

S M O O T H A L E

Round 134

LETTER GAME

1

P	E	R	S	T	I	R	N	A

2

S	U	U	L	T	R	E	V	I

3

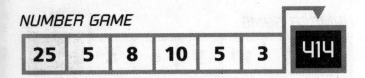

A	A	B	C	G	N	O	W	U

NUMBER GAME

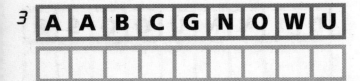

25	5	8	10	5	3	**414**

CONUNDRUM

H	I	T	A	B	B	E	S	S

Round 135

LETTER GAME

1

C	O	N	P	U	S	O	K	C

2

L	I	N	P	L	O	T	A	B

3

N	E	L	L	O	W	T	A	S

NUMBER GAME

100	50	7	9	8	9	521

CONUNDRUM

G	A	R	D	E	N	H	A	Y

Round 136

LETTER GAME

1 | C | O | R | O | T | A | M | D | E |

2 | Z | E | C | T | I | R | U | E | A |

3 | C | H | I | P | S | P | E | A | S |

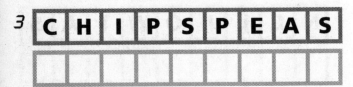

NUMBER GAME

| 75 | 8 | 4 | 5 | 10 | 8 | **933** |

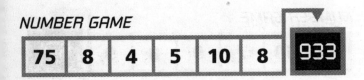

CONUNDRUM

| I | R | A | N | D | I | N | G | O |

LETTER GAME

1

D	E	T	R	O	V	E	X	A

2

P	N	C	H	R	O	E	D	A

3

T	H	E	O	N	P	A	N	R

NUMBER GAME

25	100	50	75	10	10	306

CONUNDRUM

D	E	A	T	H	S	U	X	E

Round 138

LETTER GAME

1 | R | O | P | E | R | A | W | S | H |

2 | S | H | U | W | E | R | O | A | E |

3 | P | A | S | D | E | P | A | T | E |

NUMBER GAME

| 25 | 6 | 2 | 3 | 2 | 4 | **854** |

CONUNDRUM

| S | I | M | I | A | N | T | O | Y |

Round 139

LETTER GAME

1 | T | T | N | M | E | T | R | A | E |

2 | W | O | M | T | E | R | L | O | S |

3 | Y | E | K | A | S | E | P | A | S |

NUMBER GAME

| 25 | 75 | 100 | 3 | 7 | 8 | **743** |

CONUNDRUM

| A | B | A | D | E | D | I | C | T |

Round 140

LETTER GAME

1

M	I	L	I	T	E	F	X	E

2

L	I	M	U	S	T	A	T	E

3

S	T	K	T	R	I	E	N	I

NUMBER GAME

75	4	8	9	10	9	929

CONUNDRUM

D	I	E	S	E	L	R	O	D

Round 141

LETTER GAME

1 L U B L I N E T S

2 S P E C A K N A M

3 W H O T E R I E S

NUMBER GAME

| 4 | 7 | 10 | 4 | 5 | 5 | 835 |

CONUNDRUM

Q U I T E S E X I

Round 142

LETTER GAME

1

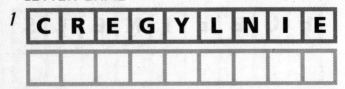

C	R	E	G	Y	L	N	I	E

2

P	U	R	H	I	L	E	S	R

3

S	N	O	R	G	E	A	D	U

NUMBER GAME

50	75	9	8	3	7	**511**

CONUNDRUM

I	B	I	N	E	L	V	I	S

Round 143

LETTER GAME

1

C	I	F	C	E	I	P	S	T

2

S	A	W	A	L	I	D	E	S

3

W	I	N	X	O	C	A	S	T

NUMBER GAME

25	7	3	4	1	2	**366**

CONUNDRUM

I	N	T	O	L	O	C	A	L

Round 144

LETTER GAME

1

S	R	E	A	M	T	B	E	W

2

L	A	R	N	A	B	C	E	T

3

T	R	A	L	I	S	P	M	Y

NUMBER GAME

100	75	25	6	4	9		840

CONUNDRUM

N	I	M	B	L	G	E	R	T

Round 145

LETTER GAME

1 P L A I S H O T A

2 K C E E R A T A R

3 I N S E C H A D T

NUMBER GAME

50	8	8	4	5	6	**772**

CONUNDRUM

Z E R O D E N I M

Round 146

LETTER GAME

1
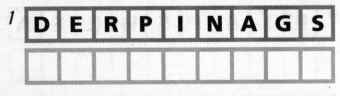

D	E	R	P	I	N	A	G	S

2
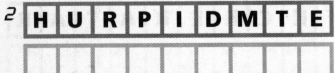

H	U	R	P	I	D	M	T	E

3
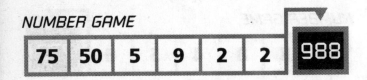

P	I	L	L	E	T	U	M	G

NUMBER GAME

75	50	5	9	2	2	988

CONUNDRUM

M	O	T	H	L	I	C	K	S

Round 147

LETTER GAME

1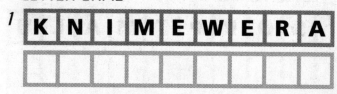
K N I M E W E R A

2
H I N D A R C A T

3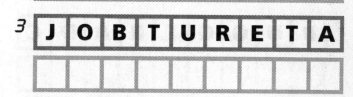
J O B T U R E T A

NUMBER GAME

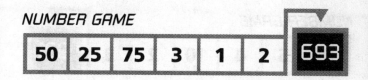

| 50 | 25 | 75 | 3 | 1 | 2 | **693** |

CONUNDRUM

H A D S T R E E T

Round 148

LETTER GAME

1

S	O	P	P	T	M	A	L	U

2

M	O	S	S	R	G	E	A	T

3

B	U	O	O	T	R	A	D	L

NUMBER GAME

100	5	4	10	2	3	931

CONUNDRUM

I	N	T	E	R	G	O	L	I

Round 149

LETTER GAME

1 | A | G | C | I | L | A | R | T | E |

2 | T | H | O | W | E | R | A | L | E |

3 | M | U | N | T | A | S | E | P | O |

NUMBER GAME

| 25 | 4 | 7 | 8 | 5 | 9 | **876** |

CONUNDRUM

| L | E | F | T | E | A | R | T | H |

Round 150

LETTER GAME

1 | H | O | F | R | L | A | D | Y | O |

| | | | | | | | | |

2 | F | Y | P | T | E | C | E | A | R |

| | | | | | | | | |

3 | P | S | T | U | X | E | J | A | O |

| | | | | | | | | |

NUMBER GAME

| 25 | 50 | 75 | 100 | 8 | 3 | **687** |

CONUNDRUM

| P | E | R | T | P | R | O | U | D |

Round 151

LETTER GAME

1 C L I M O R A T A

2 L U C H E Q S Y I

3 B R U N O T A U Q

NUMBER GAME

| 6 | 7 | 8 | 9 | 10 | 5 | **744** |

CONUNDRUM

I L O V B A N G S

Round 152

LETTER GAME

1

T	R	E	D	E	I	T	Y	X

2

T	O	R	K	I	P	A	N	W

3

M	U	N	I	S	T	H	A	O

NUMBER GAME

25	4	7	10	1	8	**555**

CONUNDRUM

S	P	L	I	C	E	D	A	D

Round 153

LETTER GAME

1

P	R	E	N	C	A	R	T	E

2

K	R	O	Y	B	E	A	O	T

3

R	R	I	C	U	A	N	H	E

NUMBER GAME

50	1	2	1	2	10	**676**

CONUNDRUM

M	O	O	N	C	O	M	I	T

Round 154

LETTER GAME

1 M O S U I R Q E D

2 B R Y G E B I N A

3 K C H E T O R I A

NUMBER GAME

| 50 | 100 | 25 | 9 | 9 | 2 | 786 |

CONUNDRUM

T U N I N G B O T

Round 155

LETTER GAME

1

T O L E Z A R Y E

2

W I T R E L L A S

3

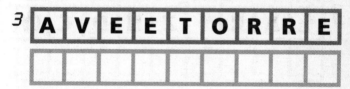

A V E E T O R R E

NUMBER GAME

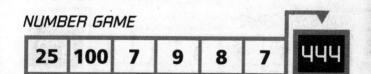

| 25 | 100 | 7 | 9 | 8 | 7 | **444** |

CONUNDRUM

R U D E R S E A S

Round 156

LETTER GAME

1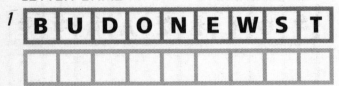

B U D O N E W S T

2

B R E D H E A S A

3

I A R I Z N O C W

NUMBER GAME

| 50 | 5 | 8 | 9 | 1 | 2 | | 633 |

CONUNDRUM

C R O O L C E L T

Round 157

LETTER GAME

1

S	A	P	A	N	I	E	G	O

2

A	A	B	C	L	I	T	E	R

3

W	T	A	R	L	A	T	S	I

NUMBER GAME

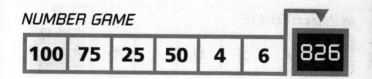

100	75	25	50	4	6	826

CONUNDRUM

W	O	L	F	L	I	N	G	O

Round 158

LETTER GAME

1 S P I M A R T A O

2 M O L L A T E R S

3 L A D E C O A S H

NUMBER GAME

| 75 | 2 | 3 | 9 | 1 | 6 | **548** |

CONUNDRUM

N E I G H D E T T

Round 159

LETTER GAME

1 S B A Y T I B O G

2 P E R I S O U G Y

3 K E R P A M C E A

NUMBER GAME

50	100	7	8	5	10	624

CONUNDRUM

S C O U T H A L O

Round 160

LETTER GAME

1

U	T	E	R	I	S	Y	T	A

2

C	R	I	P	V	O	E	R	E

3

G	A	C	S	T	I	T	E	A

NUMBER GAME

25	1	5	6	4	1	**783**

CONUNDRUM

G	R	E	A	T	M	I	N	K

Answers

Round 1

ABANDONED 9, ABANDON 7, BONDED 6
CABINETRY 9, ACERBITY 8, CERTAIN 7
IDENTITY 8, EDITION 7, IODINE 6

$(75 - 10) \times 6 = 390$
$390 + 3 = 393$

ADAPTABLE

Round 2

FACECLOTH 9, CATECHOL 8, COCHLEA 7
MACARONI 8, OCARINA 7, RATION 6
DESPOTIC 8, PITCHED 7, COPIES 6

$75 + 2 + 2 = 79$
$79 \times 9 = 711$
$711 - 100 = 611$

DETERMINE

Round 3

LACONISM 8, LIAISON 7, OILCAN 6
BURLESQUE 9, BRUSQUE 7, REBELS 6
NAMESAKE 8, MANAGES 7, SEAMAN 6

$(10 + 1) \times 50 = 550$
$550 + 8 - 3 = 555$

WELCOMING

Round 4

CABRIOLET 9, LORICATE 8, ARTICLE 7
RACEHORSE 9, RESEARCH 8, CAREERS 7
HABITUDE 8, BREADTH 7, THREAD 6

$6 \times (3 - 1) = 12$
$(12 \times 9) + 1 = 109$
$109 \times 4 = 436$

MENTIONED

Round 5

ABDICATE 8, BITCHED 7, DETACH 6
ENTWINING 9, TWINNING 8, WINNING 7
PROFANITY 9, TOPIARY 7, RATIFY 6

$(8 + 6) \times 50 = 700$
$25 + 5 + 5 = 35$
$700 + 35 = 735$

FANCIABLE

Round 6

BROMELIAD 9, EARLDOM 7 , ROADIE 6
OBSCENITY 9, CYTOSINE 8, BONIEST 7
KANGAROO 8, ANORAK 6, TANGO 5

$(2 \times 9) + 7 = 25$
$25 \times 25 = 625$
$625 + (9 \times 4) = 661$

BANISHING

Round 7

ABROGATES 9, SABOTAGE 8, STORAGE 7
CAFETERIA 9, FACETIAE 8, CARAFE 6
SADISTIC 8, DRASTIC 7, RACIST 6

$$75 + 50 - 9 = 116$$
$$116 \times 7 = 812$$

TREACHERY

Round 8

EXTRADITE 9, ITERATED 8, TREATED 7
RACKETING 9, CREAKING 8, TACKING 7
JACKAROO 8, ACTOR 5, ROTA 4

$$25 + 2 = 27$$
$$(4 \times 6) + 4 = 28$$
$$27 \times 28 = 756$$
$$756 + 9 = 765$$

FLUSTERED

Round 9

LADDERING 9, DREADING 8, REALIGN 7
ABNEGATE 8, BEATEN 6, AGENT 5
TABLEWARE 9, RATEABLE 8, BLEATER 7

$$75 + 50 = 125$$
$$125 - (100/25) = 121$$
$$121 \times (6 + 1) = 847$$

PROFANITY

Round 10

CALENDULA 9, UNCALLED 8, UNLACED 7
UNLATCHED 9, LAUNCHED 8, HAUNTED 7
GYMNASTIC 9, CASTING 7, STINGY 6

$$9 \times 8 \times 7 = 504$$
$$(10 \times 10) + 100 = 200$$
$$504 - 200 = 304$$

MOONLIGHT

Round 11

VASECTOMY 9, OCTAVES 7, AVOCET 6
BRIDLEWAY 9, WARBLED 7, WIDELY 6
RADIATOR 8, PAROTID 7, ADROIT 6

$8 \times (100 + 8) = 864$
$864 + 75 = 939$

SHOWERING

Round 12

STOCKADE 8, POCKETS 7, STOKED 6
PRODUCER 8, COURIER 7, PURRED 6
QINTARS 7, TRAINS 6, VISIT 5

$7 \times (100 + 6) = 742$
$742 - 9 = 733$

ADVERSELY

Round 13

REGIONAL 8, HALOGEN 7, LONGER 6
WAISTLINE 9, LITANIES 8, SALIENT 7
ABOLISHED 9, DISABLE 7, BEHOLD 6

$(10 \times 25) - 8 = 242$
$242 \times 3 = 726$
$726 + (10/2) = 731$

PSYCHOTIC

Round 14

CRINOLINE 9, INCLINER 8, ONEIRIC 7
WHITEBAIT 9, TIBIAE 6, HABIT 5
WALKOVER 8, LEVATOR 7, TRAVEL 6

$8 + (3 \times 2) = 14$
$(6 \times 7) \times 14 = 588$
$588 + 3 = 591$

PETROLEUM

Round 15

RAINCOAT 8, OCARINA 7, RATION 6
LAKESIDE 8, LEASHED 7, LADIES 6
PROGNOSIS 9, SPOORING 8, POISONS 7

$(6 \times 6) - (10 + 1) = 25$
$25 \times 25 = 625$
$625 + 3 = 628$

REPEALING

Round 16

SAILBOAT 8, SOLATIA 7, AFLOAT 6
CALIBRATE 9, BACTERIA 8, ARTICLE 7
VELODROME 9, VROOMED 7, LOOMED 6

$(100 + 25) - (9 - 4) = 120$
$120 \times 8 = 960$
$960 - 4 = 956$

INSTIGATE

Round 17

BREAKDOWN 9, BEADWORK 8, BROWNED 7
ANGRIEST 8, STINGER 7, TAXING 6
PROBATED 8, READOPT 7, WARPED 6

$(8 + 1) \times 75 = 675$
$5 \times (2 + 2) = 20$
$675 + 20 = 695$

FEROCIOUS

Round 18

TAILGATE 8, AGITATE 7, LIGATE 6
ABSINTHE 8, LESBIAN 7, LISTEN 6
IMAGINED 8, HEADING 7, MAIDEN 6

$100 + 50 - 6 = 144$
$144 \times 3 = 432$
$432 - (75/25) = 429$

BLACKENED

Round 19

SAINTDOM 8, MASTOID 7, VOMITS 6
FALSEHOOD 9, SELFHOOD 8, SEAFOOD 7
HAIRSPRAY 9, PARIAHS 7, PARISH 6

$(50 + 7) \times 10 = 570$
$570 - (8 - 2) = 564$

EMBODYING

Round 20

RATEPAYER 9, TAPERER 7, RETYPE 6
UNDERSEA 8, WARDENS 7, WANDER 6
ABSURDITY 9, BUSTARD 7, TURBID 6

$(8 + 6) \times 50 = 700$
$(7 \times 5) - 6 = 29$
$700 + 29 = 729$

MENTALITY

Round 21

MEDICAL 7, MALICE 6, EDICT 5
DRIVEWAY 8, WAVIER 6, JAWED 5
SALTPETRE 9, SPLATTER 8, LETTERS 7

$(75 + 25) - (6 + 2) = 92$
$92 \times 9 = 828$
$828 + 2 = 830$

CONSCIOUS

Round 22

NAVIGABLE 9, GAINABLE 8, LEAVING 7
LABOURED 8, BURGLED 7, ORDEAL 6
RAWHIDE 7, HAWKER 6, WREAK 5

$4 \times 5 \times 4 = 80$
$(80 + 2) \times 8 = 656$
$656 + 1 = 657$

GERIATRIC

Round 23

BOOKSHELF 9, BEFOOLS 7, BLOKES 6
TALISMAN 8, STAMINA 7, AWAITS 6
HORTENSIA 9, NOTARIES 8, HORNETS 7

$(3 + 4) \times (3 + 2) = 35$
$35 \times 25 = 875$
$875 + 7 = 882$

ASTRONAUT

Round 24

HOUSEMAID 9, MADHOUSE 8, HIDEOUS 7
ACCLIMATE 9, ACCLAIM 7, MALICE 6
PRIMROSE 8, EMPORIA 7, PRIMER 6

$(75/5) \times 6 = 90$
$90 \times 6 = 540$
$540 + 1 + 1 = 542$

PROPOSING

Round 25

REALISTIC 9, RECITALS 8, ECLAIRS 7
CAMPFIRE 8, PRIMATE 7, ARMPIT 6
SALVATION 9, VALONIAS 8, VALIANT 7

$(9 + 7) \times 50 = 800$
$25 + 5 - 2 = 28$
$800 + 28 = 828$

HESITANCY

Round 26

TANDOORI 8, OVATION 7, ORDAIN 6
DESECRATE 9, DECREASE 8, CREATED 7
QUANTITY 8, ANNUITY 7, QUAINT 6

$75 + 50 + 2 = 127$
$127 \times 3 = 381$
$381 + 25 + 1 = 407$

SUSPECTED

Round 27

REARWARD 8, AWARDER 7, RETARD 6
CREOSOTES 9, SCOOTERS 8, STEREOS 7
OBLIGATE 8, BLOATER 7, GARBLE 6

$(4 \times 25) - 5 = 95$
$9 \times 95 = 855$
$855 - (6 + 1) = 848$

INCUBATOR

Round 28

PURIFIED 8, PUFFIER 7, DIFFER 6
TRAGEDIAN 9, DRAINAGE 8, READING 7
SANDFLIES 9, ISLANDS 7, SNAILS 6

50 + 4 = 54
10 + 7 + 1 = 18
54 x 18 = 972

PANDERING

Round 29

BONEMEAL 8, BOATMEN 7, LAMENT 6
PRICKLIER 9, PRICKIER 8, PICKLER 7
REBOOTING 9, ROOTING 7, IGNORE 6

100 – 10 = 90
(50/10) + 1 + 1 = 7
90 x 7 = 630

PROMOTION

Round 30

LANDLORD 8, ADORNED 7, LADDER 6
ACOUSTIC 8, CAUSTIC 7, CACTUS 6
ASTERISK 8, WARIEST 7, STAKES 6

100 + 75 + 2 = 177
177 x 4 = 708
708 – 25 = 683

HORRIFIED

Round 31

CANDLELIT 9, CEDILLA 7, CALLED 6
RECEPTION 9, ERECTION 8, PIONEER 7
DOUGHIEST 9, HIDEOUTS 8, SHOUTED 7

100 – 25 + 7 = 82
82 x 7 = 574
574 + 4 = 578

SCRAWNIER

Round 32

SAVELOYS 8, SOLVATE 7, VASTLY 6
SLOPPIER 8, RIPPLES 7, SAILOR 6
FANLIGHT 8, HEATING 7, FLANGE 6

$3 \times 5 \times 7 = 105$
$105 + 4 + 2 = 111$
$111 \times 9 = 999$

DOMINATED

Round 33

ADAPTIVE 8, AVIATED 7, DATIVE 6
STABILES 8, ELASTIC 7, BEASTS 6
RECLUSIVE 9, VERSICLE 8, SERVILE 7

$(100 + 50) \times 7 = 1050$
$75 + 25 + 8 = 108$
$1050 - 108 = 942$

UNLOADING

Round 34

BLISTERED 9, BRISTLED 8, TREBLES 7
IMMATURE 8, MEATIER 7, ATRIUM 6
OBSTACLE 8, TOWABLE 7, CLOSET 6

$10 + 10 + 7 = 27$
$27 \times 9 = 243$
$243 + 1 = 244$

VALIDATED

Round 35

JACONET 7, DEACON 6, CANOE 5
CAHOOTS 7, STARCH 6, TORSO 5
SQUIRTER 8, RECRUIT 7, CRUISE 6

$5 \times 75 = 375$
$(50/5) + 1 = 11$
$375 + 11 = 386$

MODIFYING

Round 36

DEERSKIN 8, KINDEST 7, TINKER 6
ENDURABLE 9, LAUNDER 7, BURNED 6
PARROTED 8, ADAPTOR 7, DEPART 6

$(3 \times 3) + 2 = 11$
$(75 + 1) \times 11 = 836$
$836 + 100 = 936$

EXTRICATE

Round 37

SCHOONER 8, CHOOSER 7, HERONS 6
ADORNMENT 9, ORNAMENT 8, MORDENT 7
TARANTULA 9, TARLATAN 8, NATURAL 7

$75 + 10 + 10 + 9 = 104$
$104 \times (100/25) = 416$

SANCTUARY

Round 38

HANDSOME 8, DAEMONS 7, DOMAIN 6
UNDERHAND 9, UNHANDED 8, HUNDRED 7
BIVOUACED 9, COUVADE 7, ADVICE 6

$3 \times (3 + 6) = 27$
$27 \times 25 = 675$
$675 - 8 = 667$

SOLILOQUY

Round 39

REFINANCE 9, FIANCEE 7, REFACE 6
DOGMATIC 8, AGOUTI 6, ADMIT 5
PREACHED 8, CHIRPED 7, HARPED 6

$(9 + 5) \times 8 = 112$
$112 + 2 = 114$
$114 \times (9 - 4) = 570$

TERRIFIED

Round 40

SCIMITAR 8, SATIRIC 7, RACISM 6
AEROBATIC 9, BACTERIA 8, AIRBOAT 7
TATTOOED 8, ODONATE 7, TOTTED 6

$(10 + 1) \times 75 = 825$
$4 \times 4 = 16$
$825 + 16 = 841$

PRAGMATIC

Round 41

PURCHASE 8, ACCUSER 7, PUSHER 6
KEEPABLE 8, BLEAKER 7, BEAKER 6
MAGNETISE 9, STEAMING 8, TEASING 7

$25 - (8 + 7) = 10$
$10 \times (50 + 5) = 550$
$550 - 7 = 543$

REPORTING

Round 42

BUREAUX 7, BUREAU 6, BUYER 5
REFUTABLE 9, FEATURE 7, BEATER 6
EPONYMOUS 9, SPUMONE 7, MONEYS 6

8 x 9 x 10 = 720
(3 + 4) x 2 = 14
720 + 14 = 734

SENSATION

Round 43

QUAVERING 9, VINEGAR 7, QUIVER 6
GUITARIST 9, GUITARS 7, ARTIST 6
CURTAILED 9, ARTICLED 8, RECITAL 7

9 x 9 = 81
81 x 8 = 648
648 − 5 = 643

AFFLUENCE

Round 44

POULTICE 8, COMPUTE 7, POETIC 6
LAPSTONE 8, POLENTA 7, PLANET 6
CONQUEROR 9, ENCORE 6, QUEER 5

100 − 8 = 92
(75/25) x 92 = 276
276 − 10 = 266

ELONGATED

Round 45

REGIONAL 8, RAILING 7, LINGER 6
DYSLEXIC 8, SEXILY 6, DISCO 5
FARMHAND 8, HEADMAN 7, FRAMED 6

7 + 7 + 2 = 16
16 x 50 = 800
800 + (5 x 4) = 820

PROSTRATE

Round 46

SCRAPING 8, RASPING 7, PRANGS 6
BLUEGRASS 9, GARBLES 7, ABUSES 6
POSTCARD 8, CUSTARD 7, SPROUT 6

$(4 + 3) \times 75 = 525$
$525 + 10 + (6/2) = 538$

INTIMATED

Round 47

OBTRUSIVE 9, VITREOUS 8, BUSTIER 7
JALAPENO 8, WEAPON 6, ALONE 5
REMANDED 8, ENRAGED 7, GARDEN 6

$75 + 50 + 4 = 129$
$129 \times (4 + 2) = 774$
$774 + 2 = 776$

BREATHING

Round 48

PULSATED 8, DEFAULT 7, LAPSED 6
AFTERCARE 9, TERRACE 7, FERRET 6
RELOCATED 9, DECORATE 8, LEOTARD 7

$(50/5) \times 75 = 750$
$750 + 25 + 1 = 776$

PANORAMIC

Round 49

POLKAING 8, PARKING 7, ROPING 6
SCREAMED 8, SECURED 7, DREAMS 6
BISECTING 9, IGNITES 7, BINGES 6

$(50/5) + 3 = 13$

13 x 25 = 325
325 – 8 = 317

DISGUSTED

Round 50

PROMOTED 8, TORPEDO 7, ROOTED 6
KISSOGRAM 9, ORGASMS 7, SMIRKS 6
SCRUTINY 8, SUCTION 7, COUNTY 6

(100 – 25) x 8 = 600
(7 x 4) + 1 = 29
600 + 29 = 629

IMPLICATE

Round 51

EMPLOYED 8, POLYMER 7, ELOPED 6
REPAIRED 8, PARRIED 7, HARPED 6
NEURALGIC 9, CLEARING 8, GLACIER 7

8 x (10 + 5) = 120
120 x 7 = 840
840 + 1 = 841

FORMATION

Round 52

AIRMAILED 9, ALARMED 7, RADIAL 6
DEBRIEFS 8, SEABIRD 7, BRIDES 6
CONGEALED 9, DECAGON 7, GOLDEN 6

(6 + 4) x 75 = 750
8 + (5 – 3) = 10
750 + 10 = 760

HARVESTED

Round 53

RESIDENCE 9, SCREENED 8, SINCERE 7
DIMETRIC 8, TIMIDER 7, CHIMED 6
LAUNCHED 8, NUCLEAR 7, CANDLE 6

(100 + 2) x 9 = 918
918 – 75 = 843
843 + 4 – 3 = 844

BLEAKNESS

Round 54

FASHIONED 9, ADHESION 8, ANODISE 7
SECRETIVE 9, EVICTEES 8, SERVICE 7
INCESSANT 9, INSTANCE 8, INSECTS 7

2 x 3 x 5 = 30
(30 + 1) x 25 = 775
775 + 7 = 782

HONOURING

Round 55

PODGIEST 8, TEDIOUS 7, DEPOTS 6
ALGEBRAIC 9, REGALIA 7, GARLIC 6
TURTLES 7, RESULT 6, TROUT 5

75 + (100/50) = 77
25 – (4 x 4) = 9
77 x 9 = 693

SITUATION

Round 56

MANIFOLD 8, DIAMOND 7, ALMOND 6
CONCEITED 9, NOTICED 7, COINED 6
SEDATIVE 8, HEAVIES 7, HEATED 6

$(75 + 50) \times 8 = 1000$
$3 \times 25 = 75$
$1000 - 75 + 2 = 927$

UNDOUBTED

Round 57

TEENAGER 8, EARTHEN 7, HANGER 6
BEZIQUE 7, PIQUET 6, QUIET 5
UNCLASPED 9, UNPLACED 8, CANDLES 7

$(6 + 5) \times 75 = 825$
$825 + (6 \times 4) = 849$

AGREEABLE

Round 58

JAUNDICE 8, INJURED 7, DANCER 6
ALLOCATED 9, COLLATED 8, LOCATED 7
MARZIPAN 8, AIRMAN 6, PRIZE 5

$(5 + 4) \times 75 = 675$
$675 + 50 = 725$
$725 + 4 - 3 = 726$

QUICKSAND

Round 59

EQUISETUM 9, MESQUITE 8, QUIETUS 7
GABERDINE 9, BEARDING 8, BANDIER 7
POLLUTED 8, OPULENT 7, TOLLED 6

$2 \times 7 \times 50 = 700$
$8 + 4 - 1 = 11$
$700 - 11 = 689$

SERIOUSLY

Round 60

CRUSTACEA 9, ACCURATE 8, ACCUSER 7
BILLYCAN 8, LUNACY 6, BULLY 5
QUESTION 8, HEINOUS 7, HONEST 6

7 x 6 x 3 = 126
(126 – 8) x 8 = 944
944 – 3 = 941

INCLUSION

Round 61

ALPENHORN 9, PLANNER 7, PAROLE 6
NIGHTWEAR 9, WATERING 8, RIGHTEN 7
COMPRISED 9, PROMISED 8, DORMICE 7

3 x 100 = 300
9 x 7 = 63
300 – 63 = 237

SHREDDING

Round 62

PNEUMATIC 9, PETUNIA 7, PEANUT 6
HARANGUED 9, UNHEARD 7, AGENDA 6
OVERLAP 7, GOLFER 6, GLOVE 5

(9 + 4) x 50 = 650
(7 x 5) – 6 = 29
650 + 29 = 679

ROUGHNESS

Round 63

CULMINATE 9, CLIMATE 7, MENTAL 6
SENIORITY 9, TYROSINE 8, NOISIER 7
DEPARTURE 9, RAPTURED 8, TAPERED 7

$8 \times (75 - 4) = 568$
$(50/2) - 4 = 21$
$568 - 21 = 547$

ALLIGATOR

Round 64

RETARDANT 9, NARRATED 8, TARTARE 7
MEGASTORE 9, GAMESTER 8, STEAMER 7
PLOUGHED 8, PLUNGED 7, LONGED 6

$75 - 4 = 71$
$(5 + 4) \times 71 = 639$
$639 - (50/25) = 637$

PARAGRAPH

Round 65

BRASSERIE 9, BRASSIER 8, SIERRAS 7
CLUBHOUSE 9, BLOUSE 6, CLUES 5
SERAGLIO 8, GOLFERS 7, LOAFER 6

$(6 \times 2) - 1 = 11$
$100 + 11 = 111$
$(3 + 2) \times 111 = 555$

BESTOWING

Round 66

PROOFING 8, ROOFING 7, ROWING 6
TERMINUS 8, ROUTINE 7, TUNERS 6
ANGRIEST 8, JESTING 7, TRAINS 6

$(2 \times 7) + 9 = 23$
$23 \times 25 = 575$
$575 + 10 = 585$

DIFFICULT

Round 67

SPILLAGE 8, PILLAGE 7, SILAGE 6
CLAMMIEST 9, CLIMATES 8, LACIEST 7
MASSACRE 8, SARCASM 7, CRATES 6

$(7 + 3) \times 10 = 100$
$(6 \times 100) - 8 = 592$

RELOCATED

Round 68

SHABBIEST 9, TABBIES 7, BABIES 6
PROPHETIC 9, CHOPPIER 8, PITCHER 7
CROAKIEST 9, STOCKIER 8, STICKER 7

$(75/25) + (100/50) = 5$
$5 \times 8 \times 9 = 360$

PHILANDER

Round 69

RETRACING 9, CATERING 8, GRANITE 7
DENOUNCE 8, UNDONE 6, CONED 5
SHAKEDOWN 9, SWANKED 7, WASHED 6

$25 - (7 + 4) = 14$
$14 \times 75 = 1050$
$1050 - (9 \times 8) = 978$

ORIGINATE

Round 70

BOATHOUSE 9, ATHEOUS 7, BATHOS 6
SINEWING 8, SEWING 6, BINGE 5
NOBLEMAN 8, BEMOAN 6, FLAME 5

$75 + 50 + 10 + 9 = 144$

$(8 \times 100) + 144 = 944$

BICKERING

Round 71

CLEARWING 9, CLEARING 8, WRANGLE 7
SHAMBOLIC 9, CHOLIAMB 8, ABOLISH 7
INHABITED 9, ADHIBIT 7, BAITED 6

$8 \times 25 = 200$

$4 + (10/10) = 5$

$(200 + 5) \times 3 = 615$

NOSEBLEED

Round 72

BEWILDER 8, TREBLED 7, BELTER 6
SUCTORIAL 9, CURTAILS 8, RITUALS 7
JEOPARDY 8 , JEOPARD 7, DEEJAY 6

$(9 + 1) \times 75 = 750$

$750 - (9 \times 2) = 732$

MORTICIAN

Round 73

FELONIES 8, ONESELF 7, FLEETS
PROSTATE 8, TAMPERS 7, TEAPOT 6
ALTISSIMO 9, MITOSIS 7, ALMOST 6

$100 + 50 + 6 = 156$

$156 \times 5 = 780$

$780 + 4 - 1 = 783$

GRADUATED

Round 74

ODOURLESS 9, SOLDERS 7, DOSSER 6
EUPHORIC 8, COUGHER 7, GOPHER 6
PLAYSUIT 8, SLIPWAY 7, TULIPS 6

$7 \times (100 + 25) = 875$
$875 + 50 = 925$
$925 - 7 = 918$

ALLOWANCE

Round 75

SHAMROCK 8, MARCHES 7, HACKER 6
DYSPHORIA 9, SHIPYARD 8, HAIRDOS 7
BERGAMOT 8, EMBARGO 7, BOTHER 6

$(9 \times 3) - 5 = 22$
$(10 \times 10) + 22 = 122$
$122 \times 7 = 854$

CONDENSED

Round 76

QUICKSTEP 9, QUICKEST 8, PIQUETS 7
LEMONADE 8, OMENTAL 7, LAMENT 6
FLESHING 8, LEGIONS 7, HINGES 6

$100 + 6 = 106$
$(7 + 1) \times 106 = 848$
$848 - 25 = 823$

DISPERSAL

Round 77

CINEPLEX 8, RECLINE 7, PINCER 6
PUBLICAN 8, UNCIAL 6, QUAIL 5
CONSULTEE 9, NOCTULES 8, COUNSEL 7

$3 \times 3 \times (2 + 1) = 27$
$27 \times (25 - 1) = 648$

GOVERNING

Round 78

MAVERICK 8, TACKIER 7, ACTIVE 6
AVERSION 8, INSHORE 7, HEROIN 6
PLANETOID 9, ANTIPODE 8, TADPOLE 7

$(9 - 7) \times 75 = 150$
$150 + 100 - 8 = 242$

BIOGRAPHY

Round 79

AMBERGRIS 9, ARMIGERS 8, MARRIES 7
SHIRTIEST 9, THIRTIES 8, HITTERS 7
FURBISHED 9, BUSHFIRE 8, BRUSHED 7

$75 + 8 = 83$
$83 \times 6 \times 2 = 996$
$996 - 3 = 993$

DIGESTION

Round 80

OILFIELD 8, FILLED 6, PILED 5
NOSEBAND 8, BONNIES 7, ANODES 6
BENZOATE 8, GAZEBO 6, AGENT 5

$7 \times 7 = 49$
$49 - (8 - 6) = 47$
$8 \times 47 = 376$

CORDIALLY

Round 81

KNITWEAR 8, RETRAIN 7, WANKER 6
STATEMENT 9, TESTATE 7, ATTEST 6
INSULATED 9, UNSALTED 8, DETAINS 7

$3 \times 9 \times 25 = 675$
$(8 \times 6) - 1 = 47$
$675 + 47 = 722$

BILLETING

Round 82

RIDERSHIP 9, DISHIER 7, SPIDER 6
CLASSMATE 9, CALMEST 7, CAMELS 6
SHITHOLE 8, WHISTLE 7, WHITES 6

$(8 \times 100) - 25 = 775$
$(2 \times 8) + 10 = 26$
$775 - 26 = 749$

CONCEITED

Round 83

JETLINER 8, THEREIN 7, ENTIRE 6
UNBEATEN 8, PENNATE 7, BUTANE 6
UPGRADED 8, PUDGIER 7, GRIPED 6

$3 \times (7 - 1) = 18$
$18 \times 25 = 450$
$450 - (5 + 1) = 444$

ASSOCIATE

Round 84

BROWBEAT 8, PROBATE 7, BOATER 6
ONCOMING 8, MOONING 7, DOMINO 6
ANIMATED 8, AWAITED 7, INMATE 6

$(8 \times 8) - 5 = 59$
$7 + 3 + 2 = 12$
$12 \times 59 = 708$

GUTTERING

Round 85

ROLLMOP 7, IMPORT 6, TRILL 5
BROACHED 8, TORCHED 7, COATED 6
PLACEBO 7, COWPEA 6, CABLE 5

$(9 \times 8) - 1 = 71$
$71 \times 10 = 710$
$710/2 = 355$

MALLEABLE

Round 86

SHOEBLACK 9, BACKHOES 8, SHACKLE 7
LIGHTENED 9, DELETING 8, DELIGHT 7
BOULEVARD 9, LABOURED 8, DURABLE 7

$(2 \times 7) + 4 = 18$
$18 \times 50 = 900$
$900 + 25 + 9 = 934$

WORRISOME

Round 87

SWEATSHOP 9, POSHEST 7, PATHOS 6
METAFILE 8, MALEATE 7, FEMALE 6
SHORTCAKE 9, THORACES 8, HACKERS 7

$(75 - 2) \times 8 = 584$
$100 + 25 - 10 = 115$
$584 - 115 = 469$

FLOTATION

Round 88

CONVULSE 8, LOUNGES 7, UNCLES 6
PISCATORY 9, APRICOTS 8, PROSAIC 7
AMBITIONS 9, OBTAINS 7, BATONS 6

$9 \times (75 + 5) = 720$
$720 + (100/25) = 724$

INFESTING

Round 89

DEFAULTED 9, DEFLATED 8, DELATED 7
NOSTALGIC 9, COASTING 8, LASTING 7
ROSEWOOD 8, SWOONED 7, DOWNER 6

$50 - (4 + 4) = 42$
$42 \times 8 = 336$
$336 - (6/2) = 333$

SUSPICION

Round 90

BELLYACHE 9, EYEBALL 7, BLEACH 6
SHUFFLED 8, FLUSHED 7, FLUIDS 6
GENDARMES 9, GRENADES 8, ANGERED 7

$7 + 7 + 3 = 17$
$17 \times (50 - 1) = 833$
$833 - 6 = 827$

PENETRATE

Round 91

HEARTSICK 9, CHARIEST 8, STICKER 7
BEDSPREAD 9, SPEARED 7, SADDER 6
STONECROP 9, CORONETS 8, SCOOTER 7

$(7 + 5) \times 25 = 300$
$300 + (7 \times 6) = 342$

ELEVATION

Round 92

PIPETTES 8, SPITTLE 7, TITLES 6
LIMOUSINE 9, EMULSION 8, ELUSION 7
SICKROOM 8, COOKIES 7, COOKER 6

$75 + 25 - 5 = 95$
$95 \times 7 = 665$
$665 - (3 + 3) = 659$

INTRUSION

Round 93

TURBINES 8, BRUISED 7, RUSTED 6
CHELATION 9, CHATLINE 8, ETHICAL 7
HERALDIC 8, CHOLERA 7, CRADLE 6

$50 + 25 + 7 = 82$
$82 \times 4 = 328$
$328 + 5 = 333$

DARKENING

Round 94

JINGOISM 8, AMIGOS 6, GAINS 5
BECHAMEL 8, BLEACH 6, BLAZE 5
QUOTIENTS 9, QUINTETS 8, INQUEST 7

$(100 + 75) \times 3 = 525$
$525 + 3 = 528$
$528 + (50/25) = 530$

ENJOYABLE

Round 95

INVASION 8, SAPONIN 7, PIANOS 6
FETLOCKS 8, TICKLES 7, FLECKS 6
SWARTHIER 9, TRASHIER 8, WITHERS 7

$100 + 9 + 4 = 113$
$113 \times 6 = 678$

STRESSFUL

Round 96

CANOODLE 8, CONDOLE 7, CLONED 6
PHOSPHATE 9, PATHOS 6, HATES 5
SIDESTEP 8, DESPISE 7, SPITES 6

$(50 + 25) \times 2 = 150$
$150 - (8 + 1) = 141$
$141 \times 7 = 987$

DELEGATED

Round 97

AMETHYST 8, STEAMY 6, MATHS 5
OPTIMIZE 8, EPIZOIC 7, POETIC 6
CHAIRMEN 8, MACHINE 7, SHINER 6

$(10 \times 10) - 7 = 93$
$93 \times 9 = 837$
$837 + 5 = 842$

FACETIOUS

Round 98

BICONCAVE 9, VACCINE 7, BOVINE 6
BEANFEAST 9, ABSENT 6, FATES 5
SIMPERING 9, REMISING 8, PRISING 7

$(4 \times 6) - (2/2) = 23$
$(8 \times 100) - 23 = 777$

WEARISOME

Round 99

ROULETTE 8, LETTER 6, OUTER 5
THEORISES 9, SHORTIES 8, STEREOS 7
CORKSCREW 9, WORKERS 7, ROCKER 6

$(7 + 4) \times 25 = 275$
$(275 + 1) \times 3 = 828$
$828 + 2 = 830$

VINDICATE

Round 100

PHILANDER 9, HELIPAD 7, HINDER 6
KNOWLEDGE 9, GOLDEN 6, WEDGE 5
CHAPERONE 9, EARPHONE 8, CHEAPER 7

$8 - (5 - 3) = 6$
$6 \times 75 = 450$
$450 - 9 = 441$

BECKONING

Round 101

ELUCIDATE 9, DELICATE 8, DIALECT 7
GINORMOUS 9, GUNROOMS 8, MOORING 7
LINESMAN 8, AILMENT 7, MENTAL 6

$5 + 7 - 3 = 9$
$9 \times (75 - 1) = 666$

PREVAILED

Round 102

ANCHOVIES 9, EVASION 7, CHIVES 6
SINCERITY 9, INCITERS 8, CISTERN 7
SPIKIER 7, BRUISE 6, SUPER 5

5 + 4 + 4 = 13
100 + 50 − 13 = 137
137 x 5 = 685

ASTRONOMY

Round 103

THINGAMY 8, ANYTIME 7, HATING 6
BAYONETED 9, BAYONET 7, DENOTE 6
PEROXIDE 8, EXPIRED 7, PUREED 6

10 − 2 = 8
8 x 5 x 10 = 400
400 + 75 − 7 = 468

FICTIONAL

Round 104

SKELETAL 8, OLEATES 7, ALLOTS 6
EROTICISM 9, MORTICES 8, MOISTER 7
VIDEOTAPE 9, ADOPTIVE 8, OPIATED 7

2 x 100 = 200
200 + 25 − 5 = 220
220 x 4 = 880

CAROUSING

Round 105

CUFFLINK 8, UNCIAL 6, FLANK 5
URBANISED 9, BRANDIES 8, BRAINED 7
BEGONIA 7, JANGLE 6, NOBLE 5

9 x 4 x 25 = 900
7 x (9 − 3) = 42
900 − 42 = 858

ATROCIOUS

Round 106

PENTHOUSE 9, ENTHUSE 7, POTEEN 6
BATHROOM 8, ROWBOAT 7, WOMBAT 6
ORANGEADE 9, RENEGADO 8, ENRAGED 7

(10 x 10) + 9 = 109
(75/25) x 109 = 327
327 + 50 = 377

INHABITED

Round 107

METHADONE 9, ANTHEMED 8, METHANE 7
OPTICAL 7, POSTAL 6, CLAWS 5
SKULLCAP 8, PLUCKS 6, SKILL 5

100 + 50 + 8 = 158
158 x 4 = 632
632 + 3 − 1 = 634

CONTINUAL

Round 108

ADVISOR 7, LIZARD 6, AVOID 5
BRAINWAVE 9, WAIVER 6, BRINE 5
SUBWOOFER 9, WOOFERS 7, BROWSE 6

(8 + 7) x 10 = 150
(150 + 1) x 6 = 906
906 + 3 = 909

ANIMATION

Round 109

ANYTHING 8, INANITY 7, HATING 6
OWNERSHIP 9, WHISPER 7, HERONS 6
FINITUDE 8, INFIDEL 7, LIFTED 6

$(3 \times 50) - 9 = 141$
$(10/2) \times 141 = 705$
$705 + 1 = 706$

PILLAGING

Round 110

PENALISE 8, PELICAN 7, SPLICE 6
CHAMPION 8, CAMPION 7, PHONIC 6
SMACKER 7, COOKER 6, CROAK 5

$8 + 6 = 14$
$14 \times (75 - 4) = 994$
$994 + (10/2) = 999$

BLANKETED

Round 111

THUMBNAIL 9, HALIBUT 7, LABIUM 6
ADOPTED 7, PADDLE 6, BLOAT 5
ULCERATED 9, LECTURED 8, ALTERED 7

$6 \times (50 + 2) = 312$
$312 + 100 + 9 = 421$

EMOTIONAL

Round 112

HIBERNATE 9, TRAINEE 7, BREATH 6
BARRISTER 9, BARRIERS 8, RAREBIT 7
SMARMIEST 9, MARMITES 8, STAMMER 7

(75/25) x 3 = 9
100 − (1 + 1) = 98
98 x 9 = 882

ALLOCATED

Round 113

PEEKABOO 8, POOKA 5, BOOK 4
MINEFIELD 9, INFIDEL 7, DEFINE 6
TIMESCALE 9, CLIMATES 8, ELASTIC 7

(10 + 2) x 9 = 108
108 + 25 = 133
133 x 7 = 931

DELIRIOUS

Round 114

CAPSULATE 9, PLACATES 8, TEACUPS 7
DOMINOES 8, GOODIES 7, DENIMS 6
BAROMETER 9, BROMATE 7, BARTER 6

100 + 10 + 2 = 112
(5 + 2) x 112 = 784

PATTERING

Round 115

WANDERED 8, WARDEN 6, DRAWN 5
MODULATE 8, MOULTED 7, LOQUAT 6
VISCOUNT 8, VICTORS 7, RUSTIC 6

25 + 4 − 9 = 20
20 x 50 = 1000
1000 − 2 = 998

COMPLETED

Round 116

ISSUANCE 8, CRUISES 7, CRANES 6
CUSPIDATE 9, AUSPICE 7, SPACED 6
ANTIBODY 8, BIODATA 7, DAINTY 6

$(8 \times 10) + 10 = 90$
$(7 \times 90) - 9 = 621$

PONDEROUS

Round 117

SMOOCHED 8, MEDICOS 7, CHOOSE 6
ANEURYSM 8, SURNAME 7, MANURE 6
JOURNEYS 8, RESOUND 7, YONDER 6

$(50 - 10) \times 8 = 320$
$320 + 3 - 4 = 319$

ADVANCING

Round 118

PEDALOES 8, PLEASED 7, BLADES 6
BUMPINESS 9, NIMBUSES 8, MINUSES 7
EIDERDOWN 9, WONDERED 8, DROWNED 7

$3 \times (25 + 9) = 102$
$102 \times 6 = 612$
$612 - (6 - 5) = 611$

CHASTISED

Round 119

SNARLING 8, SOARING 7, ORGANS 6
SOLITARY 8, TAILORS 7, STRAIT 6
FITCHEWS 8, WITCHES 7, SWITCH 6

75 + 2 + 2 + 1 = 80
4 x 3 x 80 = 960

DETRIMENT

Round 120

TORNADOES 9, RATOONED 8, SNORTED 7
CERTAINTY 9, INTERACT 8, CATTERY 7
PAVEMENT 8, MATINEE 7, NATIVE 6

75 + (100/50) = 77
77 x 4 = 308
308 – 25 = 283

PERSUADED

Round 121

WHORLING 8, HOWLING 7, GLORIA 6
OVULATING 9, VAULTING 8, ANTILOG 7
GLISSANDO 9, LASSOING 8, ISLANDS 7

(7 + 2) x 25 = 225
(225 – 10) x 3 = 645

CHOCOLATE

Round 122

MOONSCAPE 9, COMPOSE 7, POMACE 6
ONLOOKERS 9, SNORKEL 7, SOONER 6
HOLSTERED 9, SHORTED 7, OTHERS 6

6 x (5 – 3) = 12
12 x (75 – 4) = 852
852 – 50 = 802

MESMERISE

Round 123

BARGEPOLE 9, OPERABLE 8, PERGOLA 7
TOWELING 8, TOWLINE 7, TWINGE 6
PASSWORD 8, UPWARDS 7, SWORDS 6

$100 - (9 - 2) = 93$
$93 \times 10 = 930$
$930 + 2 + 1 = 933$

TRAVERSED

Round 124

SNOWFALL 8, SWOLLEN 7, FALLEN 6
CARNOTITE 9, REACTION 8, CATTIER 7
ORGASMIC 8, CORSAIR 7, CORGIS 6

$9 \times 75 = 675$
$675 + 100 + 6 = 781$

SPREADING

Round 125

VOICEMAIL 9, ALCOVE 6, CLAIM 5
FLAMINGO 8, PALMING 7, MALIGN 6
BEATINGS 8, BUSTING 7, AGENTS 6

$(3 \times 4) + 1 = 13$
$13 \times (8 \times 5) = 520$
$520 + 2 = 522$

CLUSTERED

Round 126

SOBRIQUET 9, BRIQUETS 8, BUSTIER 7
BEARSKIN 8, ARSENIC 7, BICKER 6
EFFUSION 8, PUFFINS 7, FUSION 6

$(7 \times 5) + 3 = 38$
$(50 + 38) \times 10 = 880$
$880 - 4 = 876$

HEARTBEAT

Round 127

PASTURED 8, PARQUET 7, QUARTS 6
MORPHINE 8, MONIKER 7, HEROIN 6
BAPTISMAL 9, LAMBAST 7, PLAITS 6

$(4 \times 25) + 3 = 103$
$(4 + 2) \times 103 = 618$
$618 + 1 = 619$

HINDRANCE

Round 128

SOFTBACK 8, SETBACK 7, FACETS 6
TRADESMAN 9, MANDATES 8, MANTRAS 7
ABROAD 6, BROOD 5, DASH 4

$100 - (7 + 5) = 88$
$88 \times 7 = 616$

TIPTOEING

Round 129

PARBOILED 9, PIEBALD 7, PAROLE 6
SOMBRERO 8, ROOSTER 7, MOTORS 6
CUSTODIAN 9, DISCOUNT 8, SUCTION 7

$6 + (75/25) = 9$
$9 \times 8 = 72$
$100 + 72 + 50 = 222$

FINANCIAL

Round 130

VOYAGEUR 8, FORGAVE 7, VOYEUR 6
LOTTERIES 9, RETITLES 8, LOITERS 7
STUBBIEST 9, TUBBIEST 8, BUTTIES 7

$(50 + 4) \times 2 = 108$
$(108 + 3) \times 9 = 999$

CORKSCREW

Round 131

BANQUETED 9, EQUATED 7, BEATEN 6
PARAGLIDE 9, REGALIA 7, GLIDER 6
NUMERATE 8, MATURE 6, EATEN 5

$100 + 7 + 5 = 112$
$(6 + 1) \times 112 = 784$
$784 + 75 = 859$

BOUNDLESS

Round 132

COUPLETS 8, POSTURE 7, CLOUTS 6
HOOLIGAN 8, HOWLING 7, LOWING 6
ORPHANED 8, PRONATE 7, PHONED 6

$(2 \times 50) - 4 = 96$
$96 \times 10 = 960$
$960 + (5 + 2) = 967$

THUNDERED

Round 133

AMPOULES 8, MALTOSE 7, PLATES 6
DETOXIFY 8, EXOTIC 6, FIXED 5
ROUNDING 8, DOUSING 7, GRINDS 6

$7 \times (10 + 2) = 84$
$4 + 4 = 8$
$84 \times 8 = 672$

LOATHSOME

Round 134

TRANSPIRE 9, TERRAPIN 8, PAINTER 7
VULTURES 8, RIVULET 7, SILVER 6
COWABUNGA 9, GUANACO 7, BACON 5

$25 - (5 - 3) = 23$
$10 + 8 = 18$
$18 \times 23 = 414$

SHABBIEST

Round 135

PUCCOONS 8, COUPONS 7, CUCKOO 6
BALLPOINT 9, PINBALL 7, OBTAIN 6
STONEWALL 9, SWOLLEN 7, WALLET 6

$9 \times (50 + 7) = 513$
$513 + 8 = 521$

HYDRANGEA

Round 136

MOTORCADE 9, DEMOCRAT 8, REDCOAT 7
CAUTERIZE 9, AZURITE 7, CREATE 6
SPACESHIP 9, CHAPPIES 8, APHESIS 7

$(8 + 5) \times 75 = 975$
$(8 \times 4) + 10 = 42$
$975 - 42 = 933$

ORDAINING

Round 137

OVERTAXED 9, OVEREAT 7, ADVERT 6
CARDPHONE 9, ANCHORED 8, PARCHED 7
PANTHEON 8, PRONATE 7, TANNER 6

$10 \times 10 = 100$
$100 + (100/50) - 102$
$(75/25) \times 102 = 306$

EXHAUSTED

Round 138

WARHORSE 8, SPARROW 7, PHASER 6
WAREHOUSE 9, REHOUSE 7, SHOWER 6
APPEASED 8, STEPPED 7, PASTED 6

$2 \times 3 \times 6 = 36$
$(36 - 2) \times 25 = 850$
$850 + 4 = 854$

ANIMOSITY

Round 139

TREATMENT 9, ENTREAT 7, MATTER 6
LOWERMOST 9, TREMOLOS 8, LOOTERS 7
SPEAKEASY 9, PAYEES 6, PEAKS 5

$8 \times (100 - 7) = 744$
$75/25 = 3$
$744 - (3/3) = 743$

ABDICATED

Round 140

FLEXITIME 9, LIFETIME 8, LEFTIE 6
MUTILATES 9, SIMULATE 8, AMULETS 7
TRINKETS 8, KITTENS 7, INSERT 6

75 + 9 + 8 = 92
(92 x 10) + 9 = 929

SOLDIERED

Round 141

BULLETINS 9, UTENSIL 7, BLUEST 6
SPACEMAN 8, PANCAKE 7, SEAMAN 6
OTHERWISE 9, WORTHIES 8, WRITHES 7

(4 x 10) x (4 x 5) = 800
800 + (7 x 5) = 835

EXQUISITE

Round 142

GLYCERINE 9, REGENCY 7, LINGER 6
RULERSHIP 9, PLUSHIER 8, HURRIES 7
DANGEROUS 9, GUERDONS 8, GROUNDS 7

7 x 75 = 525
9 + 8 − 3 = 14
525 − 14 = 511

INVISIBLE

Round 143

SPECIFIC 8, SCEPTIC 7, CITIES 6
WASSAILED 9, ASSAILED 8, ALIASES 7
COXSWAIN 8, ACTIONS 7, TOXINS 6

3 x (4 + 1) = 15
15 x 25 = 375
375 − (7 + 2) = 366

COLLATION

Round 144

WEBMASTER 9, BERATES 7, BEWARE 6
BARNACLE 8, BALANCE 7, CLARET 6
PALMISTRY 9, ARMPITS 7, SPIRAL 6

$75 + 9 = 84$
$(6 + 4) \times 84 = 840$

TREMBLING

Round 145

HOSPITAL 8, ASPHALT 7, POSTAL 6
CARETAKER 9, RETRACE 7, CREATE 6
DISTANCE 8, ECHIDNA 7, SNATCH 6

$50 + 6 + 4 = 60$
$(8 + 5) \times 60 = 780$
$780 - 8 = 772$

MODERNIZE

Round 146

SPREADING 9, READINGS 8, PRANGED 7
TRIUMPHED 9, THUMPED 7, UMPIRE 6
MULTIPLE 8, GIMLET 6, GUILT 5

$(50 + 5) \times 2 = 110$
$(110 \times 9) - 2 = 988$

LOCKSMITH

Round 147

WINEMAKER 9, RAMEKIN 7, MARINE 6
ARACHNID 8, RADIANT 7, RANCID 6
TURBOJET 8, ABUTTER 7, ROTATE 6

$75 + (50/25) = 77$

$3 \times (2 + 1) = 9$

$9 \times 77 = 693$

SHATTERED

Round 148

PALMTOPS 8, LAPTOPS 7, ALMOST 6
GOSSAMER 8, MAESTRO 7, STORES 6
OUTBOARD 8, TOOLBAR 7, LABOUR 6

$(5 + 4) \times (100 + 2) = 918$

$918 + 10 + 3 = 931$

LOITERING

Round 149

CARTILAGE 9, TRAGICAL 8, ARTICLE 7
WATERHOLE 9, WEATHER 7, LOATHE 6
SPUMANTE 8, PEANUTS 7, TAMPON 6

$(7 \times 5) \times 25 = 875$

$875 + (9 - 8) = 876$

HEARTFELT

Round 150

FOOLHARDY 9, LOOFAH 6, FLOOD 5
TYPEFACE 8, PREFACE 7, CARPET 6
JUXTAPOSE 9, SEXPOT 6, JOUST 5

$75 - (50/25) = 73$

$73 \times 8 = 584$

$584 + 100 + 3 = 687$

PURPORTED

Round 151

AROMATIC 8, MARITAL 7, COITAL 6
SQUELCHY 8, CLIQUES 7, CHISEL 6
RUNABOUT 8, TURBAN 6, QUART 5

$6/ (7 - 5) = 3$
$(9 \times 10) + 3 = 93$
$93 \times 8 = 744$

ABSOLVING

Round 152

DEXTERITY 9, EXITED 6, TRIED 5
PAINTWORK 9, PATRON 6, PRANK 5
HUMANIST 8, AMOUNTS 7, MOUTHS 6

$7 \times 8 \times 10 = 560$
$560 - (4 + 1) = 555$

DISPLACED

Round 153

CARPENTER 9, RECREANT 8, CATERER 7
YEARBOOK 8, BAKERY 6, BROKE 5
HURRICANE 9, RANCHER 7, ACHIER 6

$10 + 2 + 1 = 13$
$13 \times (50 + 2) = 676$

COMMOTION

Round 154

SQUIREDOM 9, SQUIRMED 8, MOUSIER 7
YABBERING 9, BRAYING 7, REGAIN 6
ARTICHOKE 9, THICKER 7, HACKER 6

$9 \times (50 + 25) = 675$
$675 + 9 + 2 = 686$
$686 + 100 = 786$

BUTTONING

Round 155

ZEALOTRY 8, EATERY 6, EARLY 5
STAIRWELL 9, LITERALS 8, RETAILS 7
OVEREATER 9, OVERRATE 8, OVEREAT 7

$(9 + 7) \times 25 = 400$
$100 - (8 \times 7) = 44$
$400 + 44 = 444$

REASSURED

Round 156

WESTBOUND 9, SNOUTED 7, DEBUTS 6
EARBASHED 9, BEHEADS 7, ERASED 6
ZIRCONIA 8, IRONIC 6, ACORN 5

$(8 + 5) \times 50 = 650$
$(9 \times 2) - 1 = 17$
$650 - 17 = 633$

COLLECTOR

Round 157

PAGANISE 8, AGONISE 7, PONIES 6
CALIBRATE 9, BACTERIA 8, CABARET 7
STALWART 8, STARLIT 7, TRAILS 6

$100 + 75 + 25 = 200$
$(200 - 6) \times 4 = 776$
$776 + 50 = 826$

FOLLOWING

Round 158

PASTRAMI 8, IMPORTS 7, RAPIST 6
STEAMROLL 9, MAESTRO 7, TALLER 6
CASELOAD 8, SOLACED 7, CHASED 6

75 + 2 = 77
(6 + 1) x 77 = 539
539 + 9 = 548

TIGHTENED

Round 159

BABYSIT 7, ABBOTS 6, TABBY 5
GROUPIES 8, PIROGUE 7, GROPES 6
PACEMAKER 9, CAMERA 6, CREAK 5

7 x (100 − 8) = 644
(50/5) +10 = 20
644 − 20 = 624

HOLOCAUST

Round 160

AUSTERITY 9, ESTUARY 7, STATUE 6
OVERPRICE 9, OVERRIPE 8, RECOVER 7
CASTIGATE 9, AGITATES 8, CAGIEST 7

6 x 5 = 30
30 x (25 + 1) = 780
780 + 4 − 1 = 783

MARKETING